The Incomplete Dog Book:
Nothing You Ever Wanted To Know About Dogs

By

Dean Scott, DVM

Copyright 2017

Dedicated, as always, to my very, very understanding family

Dean W. Scott

I know. I know. You're thinking, "Another dog book? Really? Like there aren't enough of them out there already." And I agree. It's crazy! How many books do you need about dogs? Well, apparently since you're holding this one in your hands the answer is, "One more." However, I would like to point out that this one is different. Other dog books are either dry renditions of dogs' utility and nobility or there are the ones that read like horoscopes with generic information that can be inter-related to any dog and are often-times inaccurate. Then there are the ones with the pretty pictures that extol the virtues of dogs in their purest form. And this is ignoring the plethora of dying dog books – you know the ones that sucker you in with the cute premise of dog ownership and in the last chapter you can't peel the pages apart because they're so wet from your blubbering over the dog's death.

No. This book is different. You will not cry at the end. I promise you. So, you're safe there. Also, this book will give you information that no other book on the shelves will give you. And that is – the full and unvarnished fake truth about dogs. Dogs in all their silliness and all of our silliness toward them. The title derives from the fact that I steer clear of well-traveled paths, of areas that are more fully explained and catalogued, of points of interest covered elsewhere. As well as a jab at the books that purport to tell you "everything" about dogs. Besides, this book holds the additional dubious credibility of having been written by a veterinarian. There will be discussions on aspects of dogs that the stuffier and more serious books deign to ignore, but I think are essential in our overall appreciation and care of their species. To a large degree this book is about laughing at the symbiotic relationship that we have developed with them. If some facts sneak in, I apologize in advance.

A Brief History of Dogs

Dogs, being the opportunists that they are, have been our dutiful friends since Man was able to throw a stick. The first known dog ownership was documented by Drs. Hanna and Barbera who uncovered the fossilized remains of a family within the stone wall confines of a housing structure, including the bones of an ancestral canine found curled up on the prehistoric version of a couch. As a side-note, an ancestral feline skeleton was also found outside what appeared to be the front door of the habitation, thus showing the inferior status by which this species was held in deference to the dog. Dogs are also mentioned within the Hebrew and Greek translations of the Dead Sea Scrolls. *"He who petteth, and loveth, and feedeth, and petteth the dog yet again shall find everlasting bliss in the kingdom of Heaven."* So, dog lovers, we've got that going for us. Also, in those lost pages, it is revealed a secondary reason that Abraham of the Bible left his home. It was because he had so many dogs that his neighbors kept complaining about the noise and that he wouldn't pick up after them. When he heard Canaan was much more accepting and had less restrictive statutes about dog ownership he made his decision to move.

So, they've been around a long time.

<u>As seen above, dogs were present at the signing of the Declaration of Independence.</u>

The first living being into space was a dog. Her name was Laika which means Barker, so we have to assume that Laika's owner had an ulterior motive for sending her. Churchill's poodle, Rufus, was inadvertently the inspiration for D-Day when, being present during a strategy meeting, he attempted to procure his master's custard tart from the table and ripped the map; the focus of the map tear: Normandy.

Dogs present on the Titanic tried to warn the crew and it wasn't until Dog Linguists years later interpreted their howling and yipping as, "Port! More to port!" Even to this day dogs dominate popular culture. Enzo, the Jack Russell from the t.v. show Frasier had a torrid short-lived affair with Gidget, the Chihuahua from the Taco Bell commercials, the tabloids combining their names and forever immortalizing the couple as Gidzo.

But, why do we have this kinship with them?

We get the privilege of picking up their poop, vacuuming tumbleweed-sized hairballs, cleaning dirty paw prints from the linoleum, and supporting the economy with all of the extraneous accessories of dog ownership (or worship, if you will). We put up with more from them than we do roommates, girlfriends, boyfriends, best friends, or family members. Face it – how long would you put up with ANYONE tossing a saliva-laden ball at you to throw over and over and over again? Oh, sure, eventually you call a halt to the activity, but long after you would have with ANYONE else. So, what do we get from them? I think dogs are what we aspire to be. They are non-judgmental. They don't care about your financial, social, religious, or ethnic background. All they care about is being there for you, especially when you have treats in your hand. We get the feeling of security and a bulwark against loneliness and the ability to giggle at their inappropriate behavior when people visit. I think it's that goofy look they give us and the biological adaptation of soulful, expressive eyes. We all get to feel parental and needed all at once. They love us to feed them unconditionally. They get a house, attention, food, petting, food, fun activities, walking, food and we get someone who will put up with any mood we're in and listen raptly no matter how turgid and boring our conversation. We get to be their superhero, because they're too dumb to know any different. They're the perfect companion for us, an imperfect species. To a large degree we have to try to live up to their expectations.

Dogs vs. Cats

I know there will be Cat Apologists out there, staunch defenders of Cats Rights and their integrity, who will object to some of the things said here. To them I say, "You know cats could care less about you defending them, right? They're all back home sleeping in the sun not even thinking about you. Certainly not as much as you're thinking about them." And therein lies the difference between cats and dogs. Dogs only think about you. You and how you relate to the conveyance of food. They're thinking about you even when you're not around. But, I digress.

Where did this eternal enmity between these two species occur? I think it's due to the classic tragedy of the love triangle. Cats and dogs both vie for the eternal affections of humans. This is a perpetual war fought on an individual level, paw-to-paw, gato-a-perro you might say, across the globe every day. There are winners and there are losers. Cats offer low maintenance with no expectations of loyalty or protection. Dogs offer higher maintenance but with bigger rewards of companionship and fidelity. Most people will declare themselves one way or another. They're either Dog-People (ie. Disney's Dean Jones' *The Shaggy D.A.*) or Cat-People (ie. Nastassja Kinski in, well, *Cat People*). Then there are those wishy-washy people who won't pick sides and have both species in their homes. We'll ignore them for purposes of this discussion.

There are historic reasons this hostility persists. Dogs would like it known that if cats had been doing their job, the years of rampant plague, spread by fleas on rats, would have been significantly reduced. Dogs rescue others while cats rescue themselves. To a large degree, dogs are like the good employees who keep shouldering more and more work, wondering why the other, feline, employees just lay around doing minimal purring to the boss and getting by. This is why dogs chase cats, as a way of getting more work out of them.

Not one dog was brought to the attention of the House Un-American Activities Committee (HUAC) during the 1950s. Many cats were subpoenaed for questioning, but they didn't bother to open their mail. Which brings up another point. Dog time is your time. Cat time is their time. With the exception of individuals within the small dog breeds (you know who you are), dogs want whatever you want. You want a bigger house? So do they! You want to be pulled on your skateboard by them until you run into a wall? That's what they want too! Dogs are givers. Cats are takers. Even all the messy stuff that happens with dogs are always innocently done. They didn't mean to vomit all over your new area rug when the easier-to-clean tile was right next to it. And they always feel bad about it. Cats, however, will deliberately and mischievously seek out your shoe and hide their wretched, moist up-chuck in the toe-end where you won't notice it until it's too late. Dogs don't mean to pester you with activities such as "WALK!" or "CAR!" or "BALL!", they just know you need to get out and get some exercise. They're looking out for you. Cats could care less what you're doing or how you're doing unless it interferes with their needs.

I think the dogs notice this and it builds resentment. The cats' lackadaisical attitude just sets them off and their pursuit of trying to make the cats better companions to people makes the cats resentful and the cycle just continues. U.S. Presidents throughout the years have stepped into this conflict, bringing the two groups together, and there have been short periods of peace, but invariably one faction or another sets off the rivalry all over again.

Breeding

Don't.

Breeding Part II

Okay. Maybe that last section requires more explanation. The majority of people who breed their dogs should not, not necessarily because of pet overpopulation, though that should be enough, but mainly because they do not know what they are doing. There is often a misguided, hazy feeling of well-being when people contemplate breeding their dog. Let me tell you what the process is like. It's nasty. With a female, you will have to put up with the smelly, messy, bloody effects of their heat cycle for up to two years or more before even getting around to breeding. Imagine a particularly sloppy and un-fastidious serial killer if you will. With females also, you are setting your pet up for mammary cancer later in life and possibly life-threatening pyometra, which I will leave cryptically unexplained here. The word alone should scare you. If you have a male, you get to experience the full effects of their being unneutered which includes, but is not limited to: destructive behavior, inappropriate urination (as on your kitchen table legs or your newborn baby), roaming behavior which includes all of the potential encounters with other dogs and with moving car bumpers that entails (and subsequent vet visits), aggression, humping you or your visitor's leg raw, recurrent urinary tract infections, prostate disease. Shall I go on?

There are many ridiculous notions as to why people don't spay or neuter. There is not a book long enough to cover them all. Men don't like to neuter their males because they perceive some imagined damage to their own masculinity or display some weird level of empathy that they express nowhere else in their emotional life. This is stupid. Some people think their female has to experience being pregnant and having a litter to be complete. This is stupid. Some people don't spay or neuter because they only have one dog and it is not around any others. This, too, is stupid. Even if you are adept at ignoring all the medical issues that arise from not spaying and neutering, they will find a way to breed, trust me. Did no one see Jurassic Park? Some people wish to breed their pet because of the joy of life and the beauty of bringing new puppies into the world. Stupid. Besides the innumerable potential complications of pregnancy and delivery, you get to deal with a litter of peeing, pooping, noisy, destructive, messy, uncooperative, smelly puppies for at least two months while your house looks like war-torn Bosnia and you look like some refugee due to stress and lack of sleep. Think you're going to make money from this endeavor? Stupid. You will eventually want to pay people just to take them off your hands. And don't try justifying your need by bringing in your children as an excuse to breed the dog so they can witness the miracle of birth. This, too, is stupid. If they really need something like that, rent a video.

So, what's the take-home message here? Don't be stupid.

Neutering/Spaying

As much as I would like to have this be a one-word chapter (I was just going to put a 500-font bolded word DO) perhaps I should give some people a reason. The negative aspects of not neutering and spaying have been covered in part in the breeding section, so I'll just cover a couple of additional points of which you may not be aware.

Although there is no age limit at which you will not get some benefit from spaying or neutering, the younger you do it the more benefit you get. A myth out there for people not to spay or neuter is that they're afraid it will alter (pun intended) their dog's personality. No. If your dog was a jerk to begin with, he will continue to be a jerk after being neutered. If your dog was sweet before being spayed, she will continue to be so. He and she will not hold it against you. Another myth is in waiting on some magic timeline - after the first heat, or after a year of age, or once they're mature. They are just that. Myths. Get them spayed or neutered as soon as your veterinarian recommends, which is typically around six months of age. Dogs are not aware that we have "taken away their masculinity" or "destroyed their ability to be a mother". These are, to paraphrase the breeding section, stupid comments that people make as excuses to not spay or neuter.

Neutering and spaying avoids lawsuits. Don't believe me? When your feisty male Rottweiler molests the virtuous and un-spayed Standard Poodle next door, trust me, lawyers will be notified (feel free to reference the Mixed Breed section). And then, if you're the Poodle's owner, your dog may have to be brought to a witness stand and endure the humiliation of having to defend herself when the defense tries to make it look like it was her fault because of the suggestive studded pink collar she happened to be wearing at the time of the incident.

The most commonly hit-by-car animal is not the raccoon or possum as you might think. Nope. It's the unneutered male dog who can smell an easy and wanton female from five miles away. Don't get me wrong, males are easier and wantoner (yeah, I just made that word up). That's how they end up on the front end of someone's bumper – because they become single-minded and their testicles are talking louder than the car horn. So, certainly, if you don't love your dog, don't get him neutered.

Another reason for neutering is the little-known phenomenon of Exploding Testicles. So, you don't neuter your male because you have issues with your own masculinity. Fine. But now you have a frustrated male who is subjected to all the advertisements on tv of sexy Golden Retrievers running in slow motion on a beach, getting wet in the surf, then ever so slowly removing their dog collar......then BAM! BAM! Testicle Explosions! All over your living room! It's like the 1812 Overture and July Fourth combined! I know, you're saying you can't find anything about that on the Google or the YouTubes, but trust me, I'm a professional and know of what I speak. Besides, if you can believe that dogs harbor some essence of your masculinity in their testicles, then it seems to me you could believe in the horror of Exploding Testicles!

Glossary of Terms

All other breed-related books tell only the good things about breeds. Every breed has its pluses and minuses and sticking to just the good things does a disservice to potential owners. A lot of breed description books read like useless horoscopes – so general as to not be helpful at all. And when was the last time you had a bad horoscope? "There is a good likelihood of death if your moon is in Venus. Probably because your moon is in Venus, because honestly no one expects the moon to be there." There are a lot of euphemisms used in other breed books and below is a glossary of those terms and what they really mean. We try to give breed examples when applicable.

Term: Energetic, lively, high-spirited
Interpretation: Will get on your nerves every minute of the day (Jack Russell)

Term: Vocal
Interpretation: Never shuts up. Never. Never, ever, ever. (Dachshund)

Term: Matures late
Interpretation: Never matures; will act like a two-year old child its whole life and ask "Why?" a lot

Term: Strong personality
Interpretation: Biter

Term: Emotionally sensitive
Interpretation: Piddles on itself if the wind shifts

Term: Playful with children
Interpretation: Like killer whales with baby seals (Cane Corso) or could just mean playful with children (Labrador)

Term: Has a mind of his own
Interpretation: Will resist you every moment (German Shepherd)

Term: Tireless
Interpretation: Literally means tireless; What? You're tired? Too bad. (Schipperke)

Term: Faithful companion
Interpretation: Won't steal your wallet

Term: Anxious and timid
Interpretation: Fear biter

Term: Daily brushing required
Interpretation: Your new full-time job (Old English Sheep dog)

Term: Reserved toward strangers
Interpretation: Biter - at least of strangers

Term: Devoted to owner
Interpretation: Does not like or accept anyone else (Chow Chow)

Term: Nervous, sensitive, impulsive
Interpretation: Biter. And compulsive shopper. (Belgian Malinois)

Term: Needs early, firm, gentle training
Interpretation: Good luck with training. Any training.

Term: Perky, cheerful, constantly alert
Interpretation: Annoying. Keep away from caffeine.

Term: Suspicious of strangers
Interpretation: Xenophobe. (Australian Shepherd)

Term: Mixture of exuberance and serenity
Interpretation: Bi-polar. (Affenpinscher)

Term: Disquieting, resolute expression
Interpretation: Judgmental. (Doberman)

Term: High-strung
Interpretation: Psychotic.

Term: Dominant, self-assured, strong-willed
Interpretation: Fascist. Doesn't need you to tell them what to do. In fact, they want to tell you a thing or two.

Term: Gentle, tender, kind, affectionate
Interpretation: Push-over. Cries a lot.

Term: Aggressive toward other dogs
Interpretation: On one end - doesn't play well with others; on the other end - serial killer.

Term: Mischievous
Interpretation: Practical joker. Poops at night in areas where you are sure to walk. (Cairn Terrier)

Term: Strong, independent, rarely barks
Interpretation: Quiet biter. (Akita)

Term: Does not like to be alone
Interpretation: Will destroy your home while you're away.

Term: Intelligent
Interpretation: Is on to you and your tricks.

Term: Needs a lot of love and attention

Interpretation: Cloying. Needy. Insecure. Endless attention-seeker. (Shih Tzu)

Term: Possessive
Interpretation: Possessed. (Chihuahua)

Term: Requires special care or has "special needs"
Interpretation: You will spend a lot in veterinary care (Shar Pei)

Term: A lot of character
Interpretation: Pain in the ass

Term: Healthy and spirited temperament
Interpretation: Will bite you in a spirited manner

Herding Breeds

Collie

<u>Above: what they look like under all that fur.</u>

Lassie has been a misrepresentation of the breed for decades, causing severe depression and insecurity in today's Collies who feel they can never measure up to the fictional standard.

In the autobiography *Lassie: A Real Bitch*, besides the shocking revelation of Lassie's transgender status (a male dog playing a female role) she also revealed her on-going fight against Munchausen-By-Proxy disorder: "I couldn't help myself. I knew it was wrong, but I craved attention. So, yes, it's true. I pushed Timmy down the well. Repeatedly. And I hope, if he reads this, he will find it in his heart to forgive me."

Outside of fiction, not one person has ever been saved by a Collie and, in fact, several members of the breed have been incarcerated for various crimes from robbery to assault.

Bearded Collie - basically the hippie version of the same breed.

Melon Collie - an abortive attempt by a drunk Scotsman to develop a breed for herding melons, particularly unruly cucumbers and pumpkins; this beautiful breed is not seen anymore because of its lack of utility, which makes them………sad.

Sheltie - convenient, travel-sized Collie; thought to be the result of a *menage a trois* between a Collie, the Yakki dogs of Greenland, and the Spitz; their diminutive size is due to their Shetland Island origins and the effects of insular dwarfism, a reduction in size when a species' range in limited; they are mainly used to herd the smaller breeds of sheep such as the Cheviot and Ouessant since the larger sheep breeds just laugh at them.

Pomeranians are made from the excessive shedding of these dogs in the only known example of spontaneous generation.

Melon Collie

Australian Cattle Dog

The specificity of this breed's name comes from its refusal to herd sheep since it's not in their Union contract; people had to develop an entirely different breed - the Australian Sheep Dog for that kind of work

This breed is hated by the entire bovine community and has been declared a terrorist breed by India.

Unforeseen difficulty came when they were introduced in the United States since the Americanized cattle, not being very bright to begin with, could not understand the dogs' accent. With constant exposure, however, this has become less of a problem over the years.

Since they will herd any group of bovine mentality, they have become useful in keeping order at political conventions.

They are a direct result of Darwinian breeding practices as only those dogs savvy and quick enough to avoid being kicked by cattle survive to pass on those talents to their descendants.

One of the traits that has decreased in the Cattledog population over the years is the level of trash-talking the dogs would engage in that would initiate the kicking in the first place. So, they have become a quieter, more goal-oriented breed.

Corgi

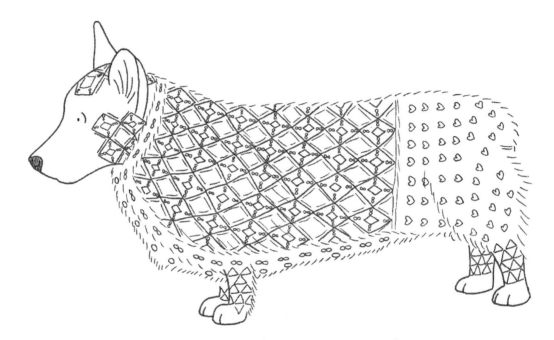

Above, the Cardigan Welsh Corgi

Two types: Cardigan - known for their excellent knitting skills; Pembroke - no useful skill.

In the late 19th Century, sweater-making factories exploiting this breed were shut down when the abominable working conditions were revealed to the general British populace. To their credit, the citizens chose animal protection over warmth.

The Cardigans have been favored by British royalty for decades and it is thought they have an edge over the Pembroke because of their tail-less nature. As one Duke put it, "They remind the Queen of herself. They wag for no one."

Border Collie

Will frequently search for prohibited fruits and ask for proper identification on encountering a stranger, which can lead to embarrassing situations for owners.

Some members of this breed have had counseling and therapy and can be found in wide-open spaces, not just along demarcated state and country boundaries.

Originally used to keep the English out of Scotland. Thus, their life-long obsession with borders.

They were also used to guard reindeer herds from the Grinch. Today they are the premier sheep herders competing regularly in Summer Olympic Games. Lately, attempts have been made to find a use for their skills in urban/suburban settings such as day cares.

Old English Sheepdog

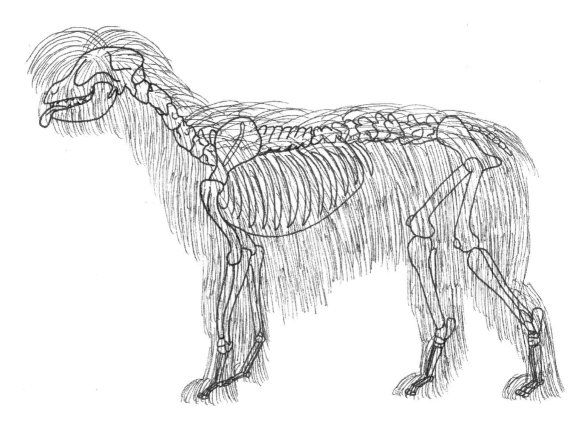

Above illustration demonstrates how the coat grows directly from the skeletal system

Not actually a sheep/dog hybrid as some people have thought.

They do not have eyes, but instead function similarly to a bat, using a unique radar sense.

They are the original inspiration for a cologne of the same name. However, the "wet dog" scent was quickly discontinued due to its unpopularity.

This breed has no organs in its body and is simply a big-boned skeleton with hair follicles that arise from the periosteum of the bone.

A secondary benefit to this breed is when needing to clean up large areas whether in the house or yard since their coat naturally absorbs all loose debris in a five-foot radius.

Similar to the mystery of Great White Sharks where no newly-born baby shark has ever been seen, there has never been a sighting of a Young English Sheepdog, so their breeding practices and raising of young is unknown.

Famous sheepdogs: Franklin Delano Roosevelt owned one named Tiny. Forever scarred by its name, he was a constant embarrassment to the administration, with pictures in the newspaper of him being pulled out of bars after some serious drunken binges. Sir Paul McCartney penned a song to his sheepdog, Martha, which has raised many questions over the years as to their relationship. There are a greater number of famous fictional sheepdogs than real ones, a perennial favorite of animators such as Sam from Looney Tunes and Disney's The Shaggy Dog.

General

Ah, the herding breeds. The Anatolian, Bergamasco, Catalonian, Maremma, Polish Lowland, Pyrenean, Southern, Russian, Belgian, Croatian, Portuguese, to name a few. It's like we have a choice for every conceivable climate and terrain. There is even a very specific New York breed: the 4th and Central Sheepdog. Due to the variety and numbers of these breeds one can only come to the conclusion that at one time sheep were a much more aggressive species and hostile toward Man, to the point where we had to enlist our canine friends. Don't let their cud-chewing vacant gaze fool you! Underneath, way, way down, below the surface, in the darkest depths of their tiny, tiny brains is the soul of a killer. If it weren't for our dog friends constantly keeping them in line, sheep and cattle all over the world would rise up and take over!

A few comments on particular breeds within this group:

The Australian Kelpie is a mythical breed whose stories describe their aquatic abilities in herding manatees (sea cows).

The Picardy sheepdog uses a minor key musical barking cadence when herding.

The Tibetan sheepdog doesn't like to use force or intimidation but rather prefers to come to an understanding with the sheep as to the mutual benefits derived from cooperation. They do this because of their belief that when they die they come back as sheep and therefore want to be treated in as kind a manner as possible.

The Puli and Komondor are Hungarian Rastafarians who were meant to be herding dogs, however, because of their laid-backed natures, have not lived up to expectations.

Weirdly, the Czechoslovakian Wolfdog does not herd wolves as its name might suggest.

Working Breeds

Alaskan Malamute

This breed is named after the famous Inuit hockey team, the Mahlemuts.

They are the only breed with such poor vision they often resort to colored contacts. You can tell when they're missing one because one eye will be blue, the other brown.

They are the heaviest of the sled dogs and must constantly watch their calorie intake to avoid obesity. There has been a lot of controversy about their past use as a draught animal, some likening it to slavery, and some Malamute activists have been seeking reparations from the state of Alaska. They are mainly used for towing now, working with AAA and helping stranded motorists.

They do not make a good tropical pet. Despite this, many Malamutes can be found panting in Florida.

The Malamute descends from the smaller Siberian Husky whose prehistoric ancestors crossed the Beringia land bridge into Alaska. The Husky is known more for its speed as a racer and lives only to pull things: sledges, finger, one over on someone, bootstraps up, wool over your eyes, stakes up, etc. Remember that should your child want to walk your Husky. Their name, Husky, has also caused them to be self-conscious about their weight, leading some to anorexia and a poor body image.

Australian Shepherd

This is one confused breed. This dog was developed in California and no respectable Australian would be caught owning one. When the California Shepherd did not sell well, the breeder changed its name to seem more exotic and therefore more marketable. Much like selling Florida oranges in California though that state grows more than enough of its own citrus. Even with the name change it remains a hard sell since the only things the dog can reliably herd are fashionably tan Yuppies.

Shepherds

Um, which one of you should I be speaking to?

The problem with the German Shepherd is it is often considerably smarter than its owner and knows it. This is the only breed that requires life-time training and an owner's resistance to being trained by the dog. They are very active and have a great need for space. These are not the type of dogs to put into an apartment without the expectation of dire consequences.

Though they don't acknowledge it, Collie bloodlines were used to produce them.

They work best in government positions due to their underlying disgruntled nature.

Like many big dogs, they are prone to hip dysplasia, so owners should not be surprised to find pieces of the head of a femur or the ilium or ischium on the ground where the dog has lain.

Famous German Shepherds: Chips was awarded a Purple Heart and Silver Star in World War II. Though technically a mixed-breed dog, German Shepherds nonetheless claim it was their genetic stock that contributed to his courageousness and heroism. The list of heroic German Shepherds is long and why they don't take crap from anyone.

Rin Tin Tin is perhaps the most famous of television and movie Shepherds. His persona was actually three dogs during the 1920s and 30s; Rin Tin Tin IV (1950s) was considered the Stephen Baldwin of the acting clan.

The Belgian Shepherds were developed as designer dogs with four types providing enough color and coat variety to attract impulse buyers and those compelled to have a complete set - the Groenendael, Tervueren, Malinois, and Laekenois. The Laekenois is the rarest of this breed, fetching a good price on Ebay in near mint condition. They can also be used as guard dogs of sheep and cattle. They love small children, viewing them (about) as smart as sheep and cattle and just as able to care for themselves without direction.

Bernese Mt. Dog

Developed in Switzerland, they are named for their size. They are descended from Roman fighting dogs; their most notable achievement was in finding weaknesses in the Hellenic phalanx. Unfortunately, even with this amazing military background and skill, as a working dog they haven't amounted to much. They have parlayed their good nature into sucking up to the boss. There are smaller Bernese Foothill Dogs that top out at around forty pounds.

Boxer

These dogs come from the underground criminal activity of dog fighting, in this case boxing, since breeders have been unable to develop a wrestling or kick-fighting dog.

It is considered illegal in some countries to not name them Tyson or Ali, etc.

Their high level of energy and low intelligence (another reason for their name) makes training a challenge. One very real and unfortunate fact of owning a Boxer is their remarkable ability to contract just about any type of cancer you can think of.

Some boxers are born entirely white and a percentage of them are deaf, causing breeders to practice a form of ignorant eugenics and destroying them as puppies. They continue, however to breed the parents that produced said puppies. Brilliant!

Mastiff

<u>Above, Tibetan Mastiff in repose</u>

Various sub-groups fall under this breed's name and come from man's need to compensate for certain........limitations.

The Bull mastiff is a cross between a Mastiff and a Bulldog, proving that man is unable to leave well enough alone. Their original role as a games keeper's assistant has waned since these dogs consider themselves no one's "assistant". However, because of their use in warding off and attacking poachers, they still retain activist leanings.

The Neapolitan Mastiff comes in vanilla, chocolate, and strawberry.

The Pyrenean was developed on the southern slopes of the Pyrenees Mountain. There are two types - East Facing and West Facing. The legs are shorter on one side of the dogs to account for the mountain's slope, making it impossible for the East Facing and West Facing dogs to cross-breed. The only time trouble occurs is, when meeting along the same path, they are unable to pass each other.

The Tibetan is considered the original Mastiff from which all other Mastiff breeds descend. They were larger in the past with prehistoric bones suggesting they could reach up to five tons. To keep that size in perspective, prehistoric sheep and cattle could reach up to three tons. Today's Tibetan is placid and even tempered.

They have a distinctive haiku bark:

Woof Woof Woofity
Bark Barkity Bark Bark Bark
Woofity Woof Woof
- Doggie Lama

The Bordeaux Mastiff is France's way of trying to seem tougher after the Poodle debacle. They have a sweet and bubbly nature. The Danish Broholmer is the only Mastiff-type dog known for its excellent baking skills and its undaunted protection of the secret recipe for its buttery, flaky pastries.

Doberman Pinscher

It's the same dog, people!

Affectionately called Dobies, their official name comes from their ability to use their middle two toes to pinch like a crab's claw. Formerly they were effective as tax collectors.

They were created in a laboratory from splicing DNA strands from sheepdogs, German Pinschers, German Shepherds, the Beauceron, Rottweiler, Black and Tan Terrier, and just a dash of Greyhound on a dark and stormy night. The penchant to crop their ears has led to many Dobies being rejected and ridiculed by their own members because the look startles the others. Older Dobies in particular consider it a fad and don't understand what the younger generation is coming to.

Famous Dobermans - Bingo Von Ellendonk who liked to go by "Butch" was the first dog to score 300 points in the Schutzhund, where competitors had to poop in every country in a pre-determined time frame.

Dobie Gillis was a famous television star of the early 1960s.

Giant Schnauzer

Giant Schnauzer:Human Size Comparison

This breed is not aggressive unless provoked. However, it likes to be provoked. Schnauze means muzzle in German which is the last thing you see if you've provoked. They were originally bred to clear vermin which grew to considerably larger size in the 19th Century. They need a lot of space and may cause trouble should they mistake a neighbor's toy breed dog as a rat.

Smaller versions include the Standard and Miniature and are relegated to the catch-all Non-Sporting Breed section. These smaller types often rely on threats about getting their "big brother" involved when in disputes with other dogs. They are also considered one of the healthier breeds, having only about a half-dozen life-crippling potential defects.

Great Dane

Common Dane

Great Dane

They used to be known just as Danes, however their low self-esteem has led breeders to change their name to give them more self-confidence. They are not an aggressive guard dog as they simply lay on any intruder, pinning them until the authorities arrive. Known to hang out with smaller breeds such as chihuahuas and poodles to further bolster their self-worth.

They come in a variety of colors: brindle, fawn, blue, black, taupe, mauve, and indigo.

The Harlequin is considered the silliest variation of the breed, having been used for amusement in royal courts.

Famous Danes: Scooby Doo, Marmaduke, Beowulf, Hamlet, and Brigette Nielsen.

Newfoundland

Known as Bear dogs (Canus ursus) in the 16th Century, they are one of the few known animals able to breed across species. Its use as a water dog seems in contrast with its large size and its development took many generations to create since there is a fine balance between buoyant hair coat and bone density. Puppies were simply thrown into the nearest body of water and those that didn't sink like a stone were bred until the current breed standard was formed. Though its propensity for water makes it a good surfer, as a domestic pet it is known to constantly kick its water dish over and require the owner to keep the toilet lid down.

They will dehydrate into a large pile of dust if not allowed to swim regularly.

For pool owners, they must be put in the house if the owner should want to swim, as the dog will keep trying to "rescue" them.

Newfie's are particularly fond of televisions shows such as Baywatch, Ocean Force, and Deadliest Catch.

Rottweiler

Known as "the butcher dog" for supposedly being kept in butchers' shops, the true source of their name comes from their ability to rend intruders into unrecognizable cuts of meat.

The first Rottweiler club was formed in 1907 and was used to try to beat sense into their thick heads.

Its tail-docked butt-wag led to a German dance craze in the 1950s.

Their testicles have been known to reach up to four pounds each if not neutered.

In the popular children's book Good Dog, Carl the Rottweiler of the title describes his battle with drug abuse and homelessness, having come from a dysfunctional upbringing leading to a life of crime. Reformed now, he gives inspirational lectures through the United States.

Vertrauen Sie nie einem lachelnden Rottweiler - old German adage
Translation: *Never trust a smiling Rottweiler*

St. Bernard

Known for its good works, it is one of five breeds raised to sainthood including the German Pointing Dog, the Hubert Hound, the Jones Dog, and the Usuge Spaniel. The breed was sainted in 1050 A.D. by Pope Benedict IX for its work in leper colonies.

Its complete name is Saint of Stupid People Who Should Know Better Than To Climb Mountains In Bad Weather.

Famous St. Bernards - All of them. Specifically notable is Barry from the early 1800s who saved forty people in ten years in his small town in Switzerland from various demises such as being lost in the snow, hypothermia, choking on a piece of mutton, being hit by a runaway ox cart, tripping over a pitchfork, petting rabid skunks, and falling down wells. This comprised the total population of the accident-prone village. After Barry's death, the villagers all died off within a year.

Nanna was featured in Peter Pan as the children's nursemaid and watchdog. The role was intended to go to a popular Newfoundland, as in the book, but she had to drop out due to bloat, which was the then-euphemism for rehab.

Samoyed

Find the Samoyed

This breed holds the nickname "The Laughing Cavalier" which is attributed to its facial expression, but belies a dim intellect rather than a cheerful nature.

Originally a sled-dog, contemporary individuals prefer rollerblades and skateboards.

Their all white coats in snow country made it easy for them to be lost by owners which is why they developed a tendency to bark noisily in order to be found. This unfortunate behavior lingers in them to this day.

Santa still uses them in the Arctic to keep the reindeer in line during the off-season.

Great Pyrenees

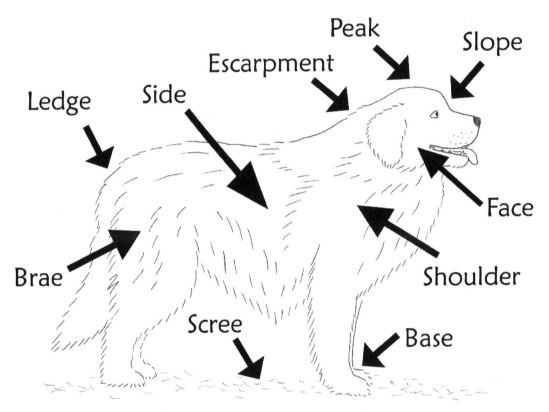

Parts of the Great Pyrenees

Though originally used to defend shepherds against wolves and bears and to guard castles, its domestic descendants can hardly be bothered to do anything but shed at intruders. Some have developed the ability to remain completely immobile, therefore tripping intruders in dark rooms.

Their more-sickly relatives are known as the So-So Pyrenees and the Meh Pyrenees.

They are thought to have come from artificial insemination techniques crossing the East and West Facing Pyrenean Mastiffs that allowed their legs to be of equal length.

Akita

These are fighting dogs, having mastered several styles including Kung Fu, Taekwondo, Aikido, and Jiu-jitsu, among others.

They were used to train 17th Century samurai. The aspiring samurai was put, weaponless, into a ring with five Akitas. If they survived, they earned their title.

Their aggressive nature causes problems in peace-time and they are known to pick fights in bars.

Famous Akita: Hachiko waited for his owner's return each day at a train station in 1925. One day the owner did not return, having died at his job. To this day, Hachiko waits patiently at the station for his owner's return, relying on sympathetic passersby for food and water.

Shiba Inu in Japanese means "tiny Akita" and is the oldest known indigenous breed in Japan.

Pika Chu is an even smaller version of the Akita, ranging from 4 to 6 inches in height.

Greater Swiss Mountain Dog

Not to be outdone by the Germans with their Great Pyrenees or the Danes, this dog was developed by Swiss researchers who are currently working on perfecting the breed and hope to reveal the Greatest Swiss Mountain Dog within the next ten years.

Back in the Middle Ages, when the Swiss still actually fought, this breed went to battle with the soldiers. It is mainly a draft animal now, though will accept ale from bottles if pushed.

Some grow to such a size that weather patterns cause it to snow on their heads.

General

In "researching" for this book I found there to not be a lot of agreement on where to classify some dog breeds. There was distinct confusion on whether a breed was a working dog or a herding dog for instance. Why not just make a general working dog category with subcategories? Then you could have an infinite number of subcategories like Sporting, Herding, Accountancy, Construction, Utility, Pool Cleaning, Lawyers, etc. Some of the oldest known breeds are found in the working dog classification, dating back to Roman and Greek times. Methuselah's dog was a working dog, thought to still be alive today, but retired in the south of France.

A brief mention follows of some of the odder, lesser-known working dog breeds that we were unable to expand on due to content limitations:

The Hovawart is not found outside of the Black Forest that borders the School of Witchcraft and Wizardry.

The Appenzeller Mountain Dog is known for its quick ascents, having climbed Mt. Everest three years before Sir Edmund Hillary. Species-centric history has kept this achievement out of the history books.

It is unclear where the Dogo Argentino originated.

The Kishu, Tosa, Shikoku, Kai, and Hokkaido are members of a popular Japanese singing group known for their addictive pop lyrics and dance choreography.

The Landseer is one of the few breeds that continues to work in its original intention - in this case, land surveying. They were instrumental in the westward expansion of the early United States after the Louisiana Purchase in 1803.

The Karellian Bear Dog first appeared in 1967 in Episode 36 of the original Star Trek television show.

Sporting Breeds

Cocker Spaniel

Above, shows how Cocker ears can be used as flotation devices in case of emergencies.

There are two types to this breed - the American and English. Their breeding lines separated during the Revolutionary War, though today there is little difference between them. The Americans bark more and the English are prone toward more dental deterioration. The name, Cocker, comes from their use for hunting game birds, specifically the woodcock, which explains why they will sometimes bite at people's hands, thinking they are small birds. No dog has performed its original duties since 1923 and now are simply pampered prima-donnas seeking perpetual perfection of their long-flowing coats. Indeed, they have forgotten their glory days with some thinking that flushing game has to do with putting playing cards in the toilet. One Wisconsin group has tried to retain the breed's integrity, keeping field trial rituals and traditions alive. They derive their funds by selling native Cocker Spaniel clothing such as sweaters and snoods and hand-crafted dog bowls.

Being the smallest of the sporting breeds they tend to over-react to make up for their size. The other sporting breeds regularly mock them, making them sensitive to any feelings of being dominated.

Famous Cockers: "Lady" from Disney's Lady and the Tramp. Her real name was Bertilda and this was her first and only film, being kicked out of the Animated Dogs Union (ADU) after multiple arrests for her hard-partying lifestyle. Citing violations of moral turpitude clauses, then ADU President, Pluto, was quoted as saying, "She's more tramp than lady." It's been rumored, but never confirmed, that her accent was so strong that a neutered male Poodle was brought in to dub her voice for the movie.

The

Joe

Cocker

Spaniel

English Springer

doesn't stand a chance

Above, an English Springer demonstrating unique musculature necessary for serious springing.

Able to leap small sheds in a single bound, the Springers derive their name from helically-shaped muscles in the wrists and hocks allowing them to literally spring in the air after birds. Breeders have sought for years to produce other super-powers in this breed with no success. One breeder in the little town of Utica, Minnesota, has spent the last forty years hoping to produce a Springer with heat vision "to be able to", in his words, "not only catch the bird, but to cook it as well".

Though this is thought to be one of the oldest hunting breeds, individuals only live as long as other dogs. One of their more historically note-worthy achievements was in flushing heretics out of bushes during the Inquisition.

Though normally very reserved in their opinion, if pressed they will express disdain for the French Springer.

Known as a flushing dog, they are easy to house-train.

Recent studies have better defined Springer Rage Syndrome. For a long time it was felt to be a neurological issue or possibly a dominance-related behavior problem. However, according to a long-term cross-sectional study done at the University of Utah's Veterinary School, Springer

Rage was found to have a close association with alcoholism. "Keeping your Springer out of the liquor cabinet," is what one of the veterinary researchers stated as the cure for this particular problem.

Brittany Spaniel

Not to be confused with the now defunct Tiffany or Bethany Spaniels.

Their silly little ready-to-please expression is what has given rise to the thought that this breed is intellectually vacuous. Underneath, however, they are only dim and lead a vivid fantasy life.

This breed came about accidentally in the 5th Century when English hunting dogs, left in France in the off-season and with little else to do, had forbidden love with wayward French farmer's daughter's dogs.

Considered the second most popular dog in France; the Coco Chanel Spaniel being the winner of the number one spot year after year.

Famous Brittanys - Spears, Murphy, Snow.

Pointer

Considered one of the most useless of sporting dogs, the name comes from their one and only ability: to point. However, they are very good at it. They point out windows. They point at random objects. They point out criminals in line-ups. They point out flaws. Some individuals have learned to point and laugh. Not a popular breed, usually being listed in the Top 10 of Most Annoying Breeds, especially when they're in a mood pointing at your face and repeating, "I'm not touching you! I'm not touching you!". Some of the younger, more technology-oriented dogs in this breed have developed a fondness for using laser pointers.

Two versions of this breed - the short- and wire-haired. They are actually still the same dog, as one needs only to provide a mild electrical charge to make a short-haired into a wire-haired.

Some pointing breeds that are becoming extinct are the Ariege, the Auvergne, the Bourbonnais, and the Burgos. These breeds have lost their pointing abilities, now only gesturing towards something in a vague way.

The Bourbonnais, realizing its limitations as a sporting breed, has branched out in the kitchen and on the Food Network, becoming famous for its sauces. Unfortunately, people are still reluctant to having their food handled by a dog.

Setter

Another breed of dubious use. Whereas most sporting dogs will pursue, retrieve, or flush game, this breed just sits down once they've found something. This works well if they are on a relatively flat field, however, in underbrush or high grass, this ability is nullified. Some hunters attach bike flags to the dog's collar so they can be seen even in dense terrain. A lot of their potential is limited to grocery stores at this point, where customers can ask them where an item is and they will lead them to the correct aisle.

There are three types of setters. The first two are more commonly known: the Irish and English Setters. The third is known as the Gordon Setter from a 12th Century tribe that died out in Northern Europe, the Gordonians. It is thought that the breed's limited ability, coupled with the low I.Q. of this particular tribe led to their demise. Thinking that the dog would bring the game back, they simply waited and waited and waited, finally dying of starvation. The only reason the Gordon Setter still exists is that it was smarter than its owners and eventually ate the bird or other game that it was sitting next to, ultimately being stumbled across by English explorers and settlers and taken in.

Labrador

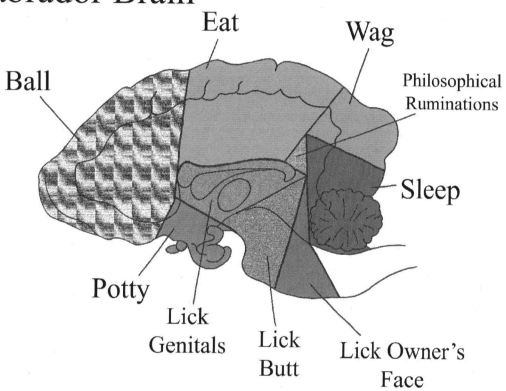

This breed has a distinguished background, being known as the Swiss Army Knife of dogs with abilities far beyond those of mortal dogs: hunting, retriever, swimming, guide dog (blind, tourist, museum, or hiking trail), military use, search and/or rescue, utility (water, gas, or electrical), drug and mine detection, beer runs, domesticated pet, assistance and therapy uses.

Accolades have been given to many members of this breed because of the aforementioned aptitudes, though they are clueless as to the importance of such attention, since medals and certificates don't make good treats, upset their stomachs, and are sometimes difficult to pass.

Among the more domesticated of the Labradors, many of their hunting and retrieving abilities have fallen into decline, being limited only to ball-shaped animals such as armadillos, moles, and fat pigeons. Not being too bright as a pet has proven to be a bonus, making them an agreeable companion.

This is the only breed of dog to have established a functioning society in Canada, having a province named after them. Breakthroughs in government subsidized pet health insurance were first made here.

Golden Retrievers

Above, a Golden Retriever, a Silver Retriever, and a Bronze Retriever

Being really just a long-coated Labrador, according to their history this breed was "stabilized" in England during the 19th Century using the right balance of chemicals, acids, and bases.

The only breed known to "faint" and fall over on their side at the least sign of any attention.

Originally considered a gundog, they are now more of a pacifist, leaning heavily Democratic.

Weimaraner

This German name translates to "perpetually startled look" and they are affectionately known as "Whiny Weimies" for their neurotic and spastic behavior.

Is called the Grey Ghost only for its coat, not for any superhero abilities as the name would suggest. The nickname is further misleading because its natural clumsiness makes it unable to sneak up on anybody to scare them.

Originally used to hunt bear, boar, and deer. Later becoming lazy, only hunting fowl, rabbits, and foxes. Today they only hunt brown cuboidal kibble as long as its range is limited to a small bowl.

Famous Weimies: By default, the famous photographer William Wegman chose Weimaraners as his dog subject of choice, not because of any love for the breed, but rather for his affinity for alliteration. Little known Wegman fact: because of the similarity of facial expression that all Weimies possess, he has been able to get away with using only one Weimaraner and a good Photoshop program for all of his pictures.

General

Sporting breeds really should be called bird-dog breeds as that has been their major function. None of them actually do any intramural sports such as football, baseball, or soccer. They were developed at a time when people didn't care if their dog had drooled all over the food before they ate it. People were confused by what they needed in a dog whose real sole purpose was to bring back a dead bird. Therein lies the why of the plethora of Spaniels, Pointers, Setters, and Retrievers. It also explains the out-of-control breeding practices that generated such ridiculous outcomes as the Bohemian Wire-haired Pointing Griffon. With a body of a dog and the head and wings of an eagle, this was thought to be the cutting edge of the sporting breeds, however it had unfortunate passive artistic and literary leanings that undercut its uses.

The Kooikerhondje was a failed Dutch experiment in sporting breeds; its name is now, in the Netherlands, used to describe any major screw-up or lapse (ie "He really pulled a Kooikerhondje!")

Another silly breed is the Nova Scotia Duck-Tolling dog. The developer of this breed had not taken into consideration the fact that ducks not only don't carry spare change, but are bereft of pockets for keeping the change in to be able to pay tolls. One last comment - for some odd reason, the Chesapeake Bay Retriever gets all of the attention, yet there are equally valid and worthwhile retrievers to be found in Tampa Bay, San Francisco Bay, Hudson Bay, and many other bays throughout the world.

Hound Breeds

Afghan

Considered the Farrah Fawcett of breeds, they are one of the most attractive, frequently employing Chinese Cresteds to maintain their coats. They are very vain, sometimes stopping for no reason to shake their fur back and forth in slow motion. There are two divisions within the Afghan community, one which espouses to have once been a gundog breed, used to hunt leopards and gazelles (not supported by any historical documents) and those that deny such a gauche heritage.

A Korean scientist cloned the first dog in history, an Afghan, ignoring the vast collection of science fiction literature where cloning never goes well. What he named this Afghan clone, however was probably fortuitous since it is unlikely future clone overlords will have a leader named "Snuppy".

Basenji

We need to talk!

Originally came from the Congo and were used as steeds by native pygmy tribesmen. Today's domesticated dogs yearn for a return to their wild origins, having only been brought from the jungles to the attention of civilization in the 1930s. This breed is often called a "barkless" hound and is known for having developed the standards for Canine Sign Language (CSL). Some Basenji owners do describe that they can make a yodeling sound, which is consistent with Bart Plantenga's findings in his book Yodel-Ay-Ee-Oooo: The Secret History of Yodeling Around the World, of yodeling's origins amongst African Pygmys. Though vocally reserved they are quite prolific writers.

Basset

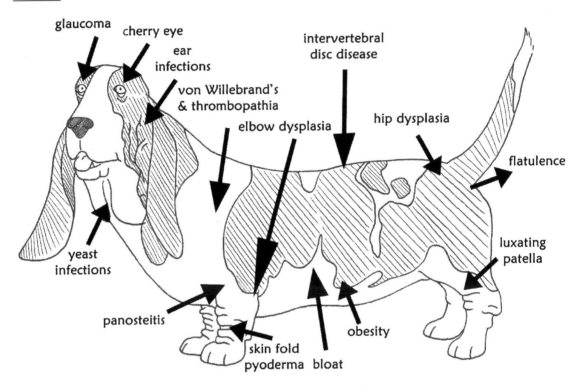

One of the best-known breeds for its distinctive mismatched height and length, large flightless ears, and lugubrious expression. It originates from France where early breeders referred to it as "Dieux peu de plaisanterie" or "God's little joke". It is capable of a top speed of 2.3 feet/second. Its distinctive voice is produced by the unique fact that the lungs fill up two-thirds of its entire body cavity. This dog's looks came about as an ever-escalating bet between fifteenth century breeders as to who could come up with the silliest-looking dog ever. The conversation went something like this:

1st Breeder: "I'll make him really, really long like a train of the future."

2nd Breeder: "Oh, yeah? Well, I'll do that and make him short like those German dogs!"

1st: "If you do that, I'll make the ears two feet long so that his stubby legs are forever tripping over them!"

2nd: "Then I'll make it so they have twice more skin than they need and I'll make their feet point in opposite directions! Har har har!"

1st: "Ah, get me another pint! It's going to be a long night!"

Cartoons, logos, and mascots abound with Basset Hounds because of their well-known looks. Hush Puppies brand of shoes use them, I guess, as an ironic contradiction to their vocal abilities. Fred Basset, the comic strip dog, and Tex Avery's "Droopy" are other examples. Elvis Presley famously sang "Hound Dog" to a Basset named "Sherlock" on The Steve Allen Show in the 50s. "Sherlock" not-as-famously penned a rebuttal parody song which included the lines: "You ain't never filled my bowl. You ain't no friend of mine!"

Beagle

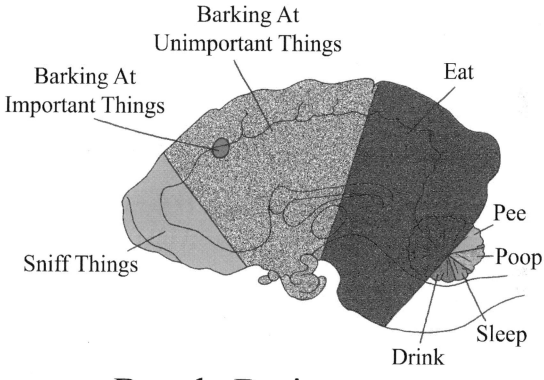

Beagle Brain

Universally considered the loudest, most annoying, and opinionated of breeds, even amongst its own canine brethren. Originating in England, where they soon outlived their welcome, they were introduced to France as a gag gift as part of the signing of the Cobden-Chevalier Free Trade Treaty of 1860. Beagles seem to never understand why everyone else around them is calm and not barking.   They love being told "No" over and over again, mistaking correction as an owner's way of joining in the noise-making. Their distinctive "voice" is actually of biological benefit, being used to stun prey, sometimes scaring hares into paralysis. They make great pets for those who are hard of hearing. The Southern beagle is larger framed than its other sub-types, the Northern, the aptly named Small beagle, the Elizabeth, and the smallest, the Leprechaun beagle. The difference comes from the Southern Beagles' enjoyment of exercising with free weights, while the others prefer cardio workouts. Famous beagles include Bagel, owned by Barry Manilow, who thought he was being cute by simply calling it by its breed name, but Mr. Manilow has always been a notoriously bad speller. The only thing of importance that anyone remembers from Lyndon Johnson's presidency are his beagles, Him, Her, and Edgar; he so lacked imagination that Mrs. Johnson insisted on naming the third one. Shiloh is seen in the movies, cursing generations to be named after this fictional beagle, some going so far as to rebel during their "teenage" years and insist on being called Angry Blasphemer and joining death metal bands such as Cat Eradikators. Ironically, the vast number of cartoon or animated beagles are not claimed by the majority of the beagle population as they display virtually zero beagle traits; these include the laid-back "Snoopy", Garfield's "Odie", and Inspector Gadget's dog, "Brains", one of the most egregiously misnamed of "beagle" characters.

Bloodhound

Above, a woodcut from 1000 A.D. depicts St. Hubert in pitched battle with a truly hellish-looking hound

The Bloodhound comes to us originally from Transylvania. It is said that St. Hubert overthrew the leader of the Bloodhounds through the liberal application of holy water and scriptural blessings, eradicating the curse of the vampire from this breed. This is purportedly why they are also called the St. Hubert Hound by a group of really knowledgeable people that speak incessantly about such things and who are shunned at parties. The truth is, however, far more boring. Their vampiric thirst was selectively bred out over many generations. This very particular selective breeding also turned them into one of the dumbest of dogs. Their brain is actually one large neuron connected to their nasal senses. When not pursuing a smell, the hound is immobilized in a laterally recumbent position like an "off" switch. They are clumsy, yet tenacious, plowing through any obstacle even if there is an easier path. They're so stupid that they don't know how to eat properly and so food intake must be controlled by the owner in order to avoid any bloat situation.

Dachshund

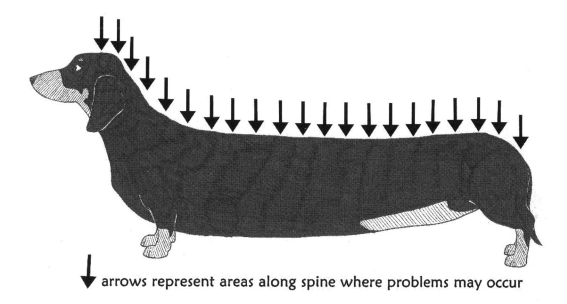

arrows represent areas along spine where problems may occur

One of the most genetically diverse breeds, they are differentiated by size as Standard, Miniature, Rabbit, and Ridiculously Cute, as well as by coat type, Smooth, Long, Wire, and Argyle. With an enigmatic past, there is ongoing controversy as to whether they developed from the Cro-Magnon Dachshund or the Neanderthal Dachshund. They are long and have a tubular shape good for going down into burrows, this now being a pretty useless function in our 21st Century dogs. They are known as a "badger" dog because of their ability to annoy their prey to death. This can be an irritating trait in a domestic pet. Among the veterinary community they are in the top-10 list of breeds known as "piranha dogs", including the Dachsa Apso, the Dachihuahua, the Dachapoo, the Dachshund Pinscher, the Ratshund, and the Boston

Dachshund. To further illustrate the Dachshund temperament there is a story about Kaiser Wilhelm's pair of dogs nearly causing an international incident when, on an official visit, they killed the Austro-Hungarian heir's priceless golden pheasants and then refused to apologize or admit fault, claiming the pheasants "said things about our mother". Donald Rumsfeld's Dachshund, Reggie, was known to regularly chew up copies of the Constitution. They suffer from Small Dog Syndrome, attacking larger animals regardless of potential fatal outcome to themselves. Perpetual back problems add to their grouchy demeanor and they are very sensitive about sausage or hot dog jokes, not even appreciating a good Braunschweiger pun. They are known to be independent, belligerent, have a tendency to bite, and make terrible guard dogs since they bark at anything and everything. One must wonder, when given a moment to consider, why anyone would own one. Remember, however, that they ingratiate themselves into a household when they are young, comically clumsy, with enormous brown eyes of liquid cuteness. Then they grow up.

Greyhound

Strangely they come in colors other than grey, including red, white, blue, tan, and amaranthine. While there are many types, Spanish, Hungarian, Italian, Arabian, their only use is as a race dog. This explains their disproportionately large muscled left legs. In fact, in their off-time, they love nothing more than watching a little Nascar. They are the fastest of dogs, able to achieve up to

45 miles per hour while asleep. The French car manufacturer, Bugatti, recently announced plans to generate an even faster Greyhound in the next five years. Puppies have been known to vie for position in-utero to be the first one out. Everyone remembers the terrible tragedy that occurred at the Wimbledon Stadium race track in London, England in 1983. Dingleberry was in the lead on the second turn when he lost control, causing the worst Greyhound pile-up in the history of the prestigious race track, reportedly taking two days to disentangle the mass of limbs.

Irish Wolfhound

This is one of the largest of the dog breeds and almost went extinct in the 1800s, at around the same time wolves were eradicated. They were cross-bred with wolves and used as spies to infiltrate and undermine wolf life and culture. They are one of the few kilt-wearing breeds and make good watchdogs if kept away from alcohol. Because of their wolf heritage they have a natural animosity to Deerhounds.

Rhodesian Ridgeback

the coat style known as the "whoopdedoo" amongst their canine peers

The South African myth goes that a common dog was sitting at a crossroads when a shaman came wandering across the plain. The shaman had been injured and promptly lost his way and had been wandering under the hot sun for days. He asked the dog in which direction the nearest town was where he could rest and get water. The dog simply stared at him. The shaman asked again a little more firmly. The dog still just stared. Upon asking a third time in a very angry tone, he still received only silence. Ultimately the shaman chose his own path, but not before cursing the dog with a ridge of fur along his back that grew in opposite direction of the rest of his fur. This was because the dog had rubbed the shaman "the wrong way" with his attitude. This is how we came to have the Rhodesian Ridgeback we know today. Also, the fable continues with a lesson: Dogs can't talk, so don't bother asking them questions. Though also known as the African Lion Dog, it has never been used for such hunting. This has led to a misunderstanding over time and people have tried to use them in hunting bear in the United States and Canada. What they discovered is that the Rhodesian is very adept at running in the exact opposite direction of any ursine, leaving startled, defenseless owners in their wake. The AKC graciously admitted this breed for registration in 1955 once it was established that they were bred with sufficient numbers of hereditary defects.

Whippet

They are known as the "poor man's racehorse". Basically, a smaller version of the Greyhound, when not racing they simply stand around with a mystified expression as if not knowing what to do. And shake. Stand around and shake.

They were made famous by the 1980 Devo song written by Gerald Casale.

General

There are many types of hounds. It is very easy to determine their utility since their names generally correspond with what they hunt. So, the Deerhound hunts deer, the Elkhound hunts elk, the Otterhound hunts ill-mannered otters. The Pharaoh Hound was used for hunting pharaoh's until finally treeing Cleopatra VII in 30 B.C. and thus ending the reign of the pharaohs. The breed has been relatively jobless since, living off the public dole. The same can be said for the Ibizan Hound. The Ibizan was a small and beautifully feathered cage bird much sought after by Egyptian royalty. Combining a swift flying agility, with which no predator could compete, and a prodigious virility, an escaped breeding pair led to a population explosion akin in numbers to the later Passenger Pigeon. And thus, the Ibizan Hound was developed to combat this avian pestilence. The Ibizan was hunted out of existence. The Ibizan Hounds had shown no foresight and basically ate themselves out of a job.

Terrier Breeds

Airedale

Above, the Royal Airedale Family Crest

One of the largest of the terriers and therefore their de facto leader. Self-proclaimed "King of the Terriers". You'll find grandiose titles to be a common factor in all of these terrier breeds as so many of them over-compensate for crippling self-esteem issues. This particular monarchal lineage is described as being "created" around the mid-1800s, inferring breeders have some kind of god-like powers.

Black Russian

The Black Russian gets its name from its fondness for vodka lowballs. This is another large terrier that has loose familial connections with the ruling class, however its mixed background with Giant Schnauzers, Rottweilers, and Newfoundlands ensures it has no direct hereditary claims to the Airedale throne. World War II saw a great number of dog losses which drove Russians to create this breed. While once a superb guard dog, it is now relegated to providing security at banks and libraries.

Bedlington

Above shows different looks designed to humiliate these dogs. Also shown is their typical facial expression of chagrin.

Coal miners in North Umberland, bored in their spare time, developed this breed to hunt foxes and weasels. They would be appalled at what a pansy their breed has been turned into over two hundred years later. The dogs themselves live in constant humiliation at being groomed like a bonsai tree. They must be kept away from pennies and some types of electrical wire due to a tendency toward Copper Toxicosis.

Dandie Dinmont

Above, illustrates the added length and elasticity of this breed's spinal column giving it a unique "caterpillar"-like gait

Breeders, being so often male, made this dog the unfortunate victim of their thinking that longer is always better. It derives its name from the original breeder of these dogs, though it must be pointed out that his first name was Bob and the term "Dandie" was a not very subtle description the townspeople applied to Mr. Dinmont.

Border Terrier

Some people say their rather common name comes from its origins at the border between Scotland and England, yet dog psychologists tell us its actually due to their fragile psyches leaving them just always on the edge of "losing it". Oddly, there is no comparable Interior Terrier breed. A good working dog, they like nothing better than putting in a 10 - 12 hour day. They can be trained to use a time clock and are known to be a stickler for keeping to rigidly scheduled break times. Being very environmentally aware, their main claim to fame is that they have earned more Earthdog titles than any other terriers. Earthdog tests are similar to SATs and GREs in that while you can do well on them, they have no real world applicable value. Border terriers are quite popular for use in movies and television and can be seen in Will Ferrell's *Anchorman*, in *Prometheus*, *There's Something About Mary*, and memorably, as the faithful dog Seymour in *Futurama*.

Parsons Russell

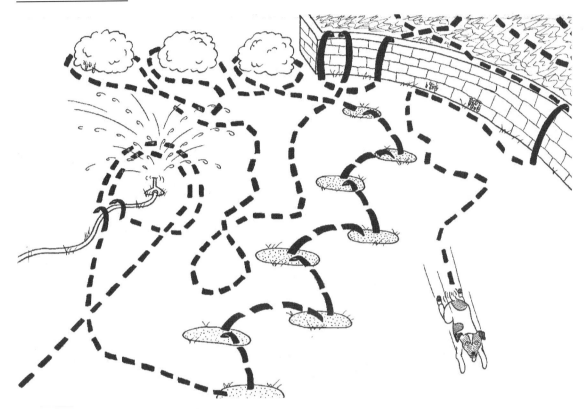

<u>Above, elapsed time: 20 seconds</u>

Many make the common mistake of calling the entire breed the Jack Russell, but it is more accurate to only apply this to the males; the female gender should only be properly referred to as Jill Russells. What you think of this breed depends on your viewpoint. Vocal and energetic? or skull-splittingly annoying and aggravating? Fearless? or Stupid?

The only small dog breed deliberately described as NOT a lap dog. They are completely unfazed by any tranquilizer known to veterinary medicine.

Their short tail is used as a handle to pull them out of holes in which they have pursued prey. This is necessary as, even if they could hear you over their own barking, they still wouldn't listen.

The Reverend John Russell was universally reviled by his Devon, England neighbors for making this breed. Folklore says that one fateful stormy night, when he unleashed it on the countryside, the villagers rose up, waving pitchforks and torches, confronting him in his castle on the top of the mountain. But it was too late.

Ranulf Fiennes became a famous explorer by accident when tenaciously pursuing his escaped Jack Russell, Bothie, deep into the Antarctic. Bothie proved to be just a touch more tenacious about keeping away from him.

Cairn

So-called because of their enjoyment in stacking stones on top of each other to form conical shapes. There is some credible historical evidence that packs of these terriers were central to the building of Hadrian's Wall built around 122 A.D. The most famous of the Cairns is, of course, Terry, who played Toto in the 1939 film Wizard of Oz. She was known to be very difficult on the set, playing practical jokes on her cast-mates. Ray Bolger noticed a peculiar smell after donning his Scarecrow costume, only later realizing it was from dried dog urine. He held a grudge the rest of his life, often repeating his grievance in interviews. Terry particularly liked to nip at Judy Garland's red ruby slippers and leaving notes in random places reading, "Go Home, Dorothy!". Though playing a dog adored by millions, hardly anyone had a good thing to say about her, some from jealousy as she was paid more than any of the other supporting actors and got her own trailer, whereas many of the Munchkins had to share lodging.

West Highland

Considered the most optimistic of this breed group, it is used primarily as a psychological counselor to the dour Bassetts and depressed English Bulldogs. It is related to the Cairn and Scottish Terriers. While white variations were frowned upon early on and disqualified as "true" Westies, Breed Rights laws were put into place to afford equal opportunities to this breed's members. This caused an unfortunate over-compensation and now only white coats are permissible, making it the most popular breed amongst supremacist groups in the United States. Canine law attorneys continue to study this problem of disparity as well as whether "breedist" views led to the extinction of the East Highland Terriers.

This is the most literary of breeds, appearing in illustrated children's books, MC Beaton's popular series featuring the main character's companion Wee Jock, PD Wodehouse's Jeeves and Wooster series, and in the *American Girl* book series. This is no accident, since they are also the only literate breed.

Scottish

Live Scottish
or Die Hard!

You may take our
balls, but you'll
never take.....
our Freedom!

Derives the nickname "Diehard" from their inordinate fondness for Bruce Willis movies. From 1860 - 1880 there was a lot of controversy concerning this breed when people with too much time on their hands had long, furious public discussions until a breed standard was finally ratified and accepted. The harsh, wiry coat makes it so no water can penetrate, making it impossible to bathe them. This coat is helpful, though, because you can use them for scrubbing out set-in stains or hard, dry substances adhered to kitchen counters, bathtubs, etc. Like many of the terrier breeds, its original use to hunt badger and fox has become obsolete and its only function now is as a household pet. Some still hope its original abilities will be of use in a post-apocalyptic world.

This breed has the most political clout of any other, its past including access to the White House, Queen Victoria, the Kennedys, the President of Poland, and Bill Cosby. They have a huge lobbying group to push Scottish Terrier interests.

Cesky (also Czesky or Cheski or Chzeskiy)

Originally a breed that hailed from Czechoslovakia, it is a less aggressive member of the Terrier group, feeling like it has nothing to prove. Because of the dissolution of Czechoslovakia into the current Czech Republic and Slovakia, the breed is now known by a symbol (make up symbol) and referred to as the "dog formerly known as Czesky". They were bred for underground burrowing work such as mining for coal and mineral deposits. Made by yet another mad scientist, Dr. Frantresk Llorak, a geneticist and known breeder, gene splicing from Scottish and Sealyham Terriers as well as DNA strands from the famous Czech nationalist Josef Jungmann.

Skye

While it seems obvious from the name, the Skye Terrier is the only aerial-based terrier, employing its unique "pricked" ears as wings. Referred to as a Dog of Prey for its ability to overtake game. It was originally developed by Scottish breeders to harass and drop rocks from on-high onto occupying English forces as well as individual Protestants. They are not as popular as other terrier breeds due to their higher maintenance and love of dive-bombing other household pets.

Kerry Blue

Above, a Kerry Blue plays B.B. King's "Every Day I Have the Blues"

So-named for its phosphorescent blue coat which is helpful in nighttime hunts. Being the national dog of Ireland, it naturally considers itself a superior being, demanding tithes and offerings from other terriers. It is said to like people and exercise and enjoys nothing more than when it can combine the two, such as chasing after people, as it does in its primary occupations as watchdog or police dog. It is said that they require just the right balance of training with patience and firmness, as being too strict may discourage it. Which means this breed should not be owned by anyone as it will either walk all over you if you're too easy on it or petulantly sulk because it feels you raised your voice at it inappropriately.

Australian

Above, an Australian Terrier and two Yorkies

This breed has low self-esteem and is described as "anxious to please". Its small size means they do not cost much to feed, having a superior miles-per-kibble (MpK) ratio. They're basically a Yorkie/Cairn mixed breed that you pay more for. Originally British, it was used quite effectively in protecting settler's property and lives from any threat measuring twelve inches or less.

Bull

This breed is full of it. Known as the "Gladiator" of terriers because they were initially used in dog-fighting, few people are aware that they came up with this name themselves. While many people find its odd egg-shaped head humorous, those who reference it or point it out only serve to piss this breed off. Like the Westie, these dogs have suffered from breedism, with the white coated Bull Terriers initially disparaged by the Bull Terriers of Color. The oldest known member of the breed was a female called "Puppa Trout", once described as an "attractive power-packed bitch" by a show judge of questionable standing. Deafness is thought to occur in this breed but really, they hear you. They just don't care.

American Staffordshire

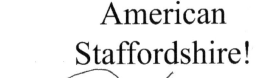

Also known as the Pitbull, this breed has an unfortunate reputation perpetuated by the liberal media's bias in reporting news only when a small minority of the population gets into trouble. This reputation has led breeders to try to develop different genetic lines, but have not been completely successful in eradicating certain unacceptable behaviors, one result being the Spitbull. There is some truth, however, in that many of this breed do not like other dogs, though this is felt to be more due to their sensitivity in being labeled as they have been, where other aggressive breeds, such as Lhasas, Dachshunds, Chihuahuas, etc. have not. There is also definite breed snobbery seen with the English looking down on the American breed's presumed crassness and low-born upbringing. To their credit, the Americans don't really care, knowing they can kick the English's collective asses. Famous Pitbulls include "Sergeant Stubby", the most decorated dog in military history and "Petey" who was known for not eating even one Little Rascal.

Fun fact: one of the breeds known to have such sizable litters that there are more puppies than nipples.

General

Because of their hyperkinetic nature, terriers are often referred to by their owners as "terrorists", sometimes affectionately, sometimes just descriptively. It is for this reason that commercial airlines do not allow them on flights without being under sedation as prescribed by a licensed veterinarian. Terriers seem to proliferate in their variety due to the United Kingdom citizen's natural tendency toward competition, with every town and county trying to generate a new, better, or unique type of their own in an effort to disgrace their neighbors. Thus, you get the Norwich, the Aberdeen, the Devon, the unfortunate Dunwich Horror, the Manchester, the Sealyham, and, well, you get the point.

Then there's the Welsh Terrier who should never be loaned money.

And the Nether Wallop Terrier from a village in Hampshire, which has a bowling ball-shaped head and an uncanny knack for jumping up about 2-3 feet in the air behind people.

Other countries have tried to horn in on the terrier action, Japan, Brazil, and the Czech Republic in particular. New terrier breeds are being developed every day, many completely unsanctioned by couplings between fence-jumping males and females of questionable morals.

Toy Breeds

General

We've put the general section first to make clear some particular traits of dogs in this category. The main way a dog will be considered a toy breed is based on its level of uselessness. This is also the only category where different breeds can be ranked based on their Adorableness Quotient (A.Q.). A rule of thumb is that the higher the A.Q., the lower the I.Q., therefore leading to a veritable raft of truly dumb dogs. Most of the breeds found here would be unable to survive without the direct intervention of humans, since they require a huge investment of time either to grooming, medical care, or soothing their disproportionately-sized egos. A brief mention of a few toy breeds not covered extensively in this section:

The Japanese Chin has none and is said to enjoy a "scurry 'round the garden" but appreciates a gambol over Astroturf if that is all that is available.

The Lowchen, or "Little Lion Dog", is misnamed as they require special grooming to force the coat to resemble that of a lion. The shaved back half of the dog just makes for a cold bum on winter nights.

The Peruvian and Mexican Hairless dogs on the other hand need no such shaving. The only thing they wear is a perpetual look of "What happened?"

The Coton de Tulear has one of the most pretentious of names, especially when you consider it was only developed as a source of synthetic cotton, the number one export of Madagascar from where it originates.

Many members found in this category suffer from a behavioral disorder called Small Dog Syndrome (SDS), where they try to intimidate through sheer volume and dramatic posturing.

Owners will find that many of these breeds are resistant to any type of discomfort, from their paws touching moisture-laden grass to having to feed themselves. Toy breeds are also known to burn through AA and AAA batteries at a significant rate.

Affenpinscher

This is the first breed mentioned in any breed book (except this one), not because of its popularity, but because of alphabetical listings. They were formerly known as Assenpinschers until that particular embarrassing trait was weeded out of the gene pool. The endearing nickname, "Black Devil", derives from their earlier, less reputable origins. Some, unfortunately, may express a gene for this behavior and have to attend Assenpinscher Anonymous meetings (also referred to as "the other A.A."). "Monkey terrier" is another reference made to them, this one due to their prehensile tail. There are rumors that you can still find wild Affenpinschers living in the upper canopy of forested areas in Germany. Most countries only recognize the black-coated version, except in the more accepting United States where mixtures of colors are allowed. Most often mistaken for homeless stray dogs. While it is touted that they are used for controlling vermin, this is a bit of an over-statement, as Affenpinschers really only consider such activities as more of a hobby.

Fun fact: George Lucas got his idea for Chewbacca from this breed.

Bichon

<u>Above, Bichons shown depicting Renaissance-style topiary</u>

Known as the "Renaissance Dog", not because of any notable achievements, but because of being owned by such notables as Boccacio, Michelangelo, Botticelli, and da Vinci. It seems that other countries of the time felt that France was deficient in canine imports as this is yet another breed that was introduced there to go on to an overly-pampered life. It is basically a fluffier poodle which not only requires, but demands, daily brushing. Being popular in 17th century literary salons in France, members of this breed have never worked a day in their lives. Besides France, this breed had an early broad distribution in Spain, Italy, Belgium, and England, being used as a barter item by sailors. Its public stock today continues to cause a lot of volatility in the marketplace. Like the Bedlington terrier, this is another example of a "topiary" dog. Their high A.Q. is based on their having perfected the 22-degree head-tilt that owners find so irresistible.

Cavalier King Charles Spaniel

Known as a "carpet dog", this is the only non-working Spaniel breed, and thus, shunned by other respectable Spaniels. Its "cavalier" title comes from what breeders describe as a non-judgmental attitude, but really derives from just not caring. Once known as a gundog, its natural pacifist nature makes owning a weapon impossible. King Charles II was so enamored and distracted with this breed it allowed Oliver Cromwell to take over control of the United Kingdom, causing the country to languish in the mid-17th century. Though the breed had been around for quite a while, it wasn't recognized by the American Kennel Club until 1996, principally due to its lackadaisical approach toward paperwork and the application process. The King Charles Spaniel is the most well-known, however there are smaller versions of this breed as well- the Queen Charles, the Full Charles, and the Twin Charles Spaniels.

Chihuahua

Chihuahuas have always been suckers for advertising

Body by "Jake"*
Canine
Bodybuilding
System
*steroids not included
In Only 30 Days!

The Aztecs viewed this breed as sacred, using them as holy food and in sacrifices to their gods. This history is responsible for their propensity toward biting, feeling that anyone reaching towards them has suspect motives. Many individuals are known to have open fontanelles in their skulls and love nothing better than good protective headgear. Being all too-aware of what is basically an extra hole in the head and their small size is what makes nervous shaking a natural condition for this breed. A popular dog among masochists.

Chinese Crested

There are two types to this breed. The hairless, or "nudist", and their more-demure cousins known as powderpuffs. They are so in-bred it is rare to find one with a full set of teeth. Originating from African hairless dogs (now extinct from sun-burned induced melanomas), this is another breed, like the Bichon, used in the past as barter between sailors. Because of the lower A.Q., however, it worked out to about a three Chinese Cresteds to one Bichon exchange rate. They are sensitive to cold, but it is also difficult to find clothing materials that their skin doesn't react to. Because of their sensitivity to temperatures, they are the only breed who has learned to operate a thermostat. A favorite dog among veterinary dermatologists.

Italian Greyhound

Another ancient breed believed to come from hypothyroid Egyptian Greyhounds. Having a pagan background, they were converted to Catholicism during the reign of Mary, Queen of Scots. Expatriated members of the breed were found in Italy as early as 5th century B.C. Often confused with the Whippet, its main difference is that it is much more likely to fly off the handle at the smallest of inconveniences or perceived insult. One would think being designated a Greyhound would automatically disqualify it as being a toy breed, however its legs are easily breakable like fine china and they must be carried or walked in a stroller and must always, if absolutely necessary to be put down, be gently, ever so gently, placed on the softest of cushions. They dislike inclement weather and need a nice water-resistant jacket and galoshes and/or an owner willing to follow them around the yard with an umbrella. Like the Chihuahua, its fragile psyche and worry over its limbs causes it to shake for no discernible reason.

Maltese

Why doesn't he approve of us?

You would think that being known as "the ancient dog of Malta" would bring some respectability to this breed, yet it, too, is fairly useless. They require more maintenance than any animal should. Psychiatrists often recommend this breed to overly needy patients with a lot of time on their hands. With their ancient historic background, such as hobnobbing with the likes of Queen Elizabeth I, and grandiose sense of self, they dislike being forced to do anything and seem not to understand an owner that doesn't constantly attend to its needs. They will respond reluctantly to baby talk. Other Maltese-derived breeds include the Bolognese and Havanese. The former is where the popular processed meat of the same name comes from. The latter is known for its coat that exudes a rich, pungent scent.

Fun fact: this breed doesn't have legs, but instead glides along on rotating treads.

Miniature Pinscher

The Difference Between A Min Pin And An English Toy

Believed to come from hypothyroid Dobermans - yet another example of breeders' need to pass on hereditary disease conditions. It was designated as a Terrier at first, until it proved its level of usefulness to be well below that standard. Its large ears make it able to hear everything and is a notorious gossip. The nickname, Min Pin, comes obviously from a shortening of the breed's name, but it seconds as a quick early warning for visitors to their house or for anyone attempting to pet it. "Min Pin!" They have their own disability, known as Min Pin Attention Deficit Disorder (MPADD), resulting in the energy level of a hummingbird and the attention span of a moth. While the black and tan is the most recognized coat color, the dark brown and tan is also acceptable. The plainer single-coated dogs are basically chihuahuas. Breeders will tell you that it worked as a ratter in Germany, but truth be told, rats found their attempts to be hilarious. The Min Pin club in Germany is called the Zwerg and is run by people of small stature trying to look tougher. Some will try to persuade you that the English Toy Terrier is a separate breed. It's a Min Pin. Come on! Just look at it!

Papillon

Known as the "Butterfly" dog, it starts out as a hairless chinese crested, forms a cocoon around 3 - 5 days of age, and emerges in the familiar form of the Papillon. Its ability to escape from any situation was immortalized in the 1973 film, *Papillon*, starring Steve McQueen. Some snobbish breed books throw them in under the title of Continental Toy Spaniels. This is erroneous as the Papillon is well-known to never eat breakfast. Marie Antoinette loved this dog but was ultimately betrayed by it at her trial. Believed to have made its way from France to England and ultimately to the United States in the cargo-hold of ships, unknowingly by the crew. In the New World, people had not developed any defense against its high A.Q., thus allowing its numbers to proliferate. This breed loves to play with others, being especially fond of board games.

Pekingese

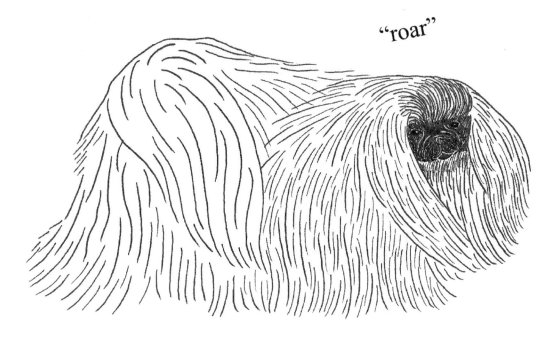

"roar"

There is a story that tells of a lion who fell in love with a marmoset. Ah Chu, patron saint of animals, shrunk the lion in size, thus allowing love to flourish and produce generations of asthmatic, over-weight dust-collectors. This romantic rendition of this breed's background belies that fact that it is the most useless of breeds. Another undeserved appellation is that of "Lion Dog", as it was believed to protect the Chinese Emperor in the after-life. This dog isn't even able to protect its own feelings and can only be remotely useful as a tripping hazard. Again, this breed would not exist without the patronage of Chinese Imperials and was a sacred dog of the Tang Dynasty, known for its invention of fruit-flavored breakfast drinks. Its sad expression is due to what we've done to this breed's ability to breathe and it is incapable of running more than three feet without the use of an inhaler.

Pomeranian

As mentioned before, this is the only breed know to spontaneously generate from the sheddings of Collies. It is basically a fluffier chihuahua (which you can discover if you ever have a free afternoon and an electric trimmer). Its only "skill" is in producing a barrage of shrill yapping which is thought to deter burglars. In a survey of those in prison for breaking and entering (B&E), however, Pomeranians are referred to as one of the most "kickable" breeds. They are a study in contrasts, having the lowest brain:body size ratio - they are trainable as long as commands are limited to one-syllable words repeated up to twenty times. Their body mass is also made up mostly of fur, having a 4:1 ratio of fur to actual dog. Though its background comes from a list of useful dogs, such as Spitzes, Elkhound, Chow Chow, and Samoyeds, the first thing to go when they were bred down in size was their usefulness. Queen Victoria loved to use them as shuttlecocks in games of badminton. This is another breed that suffers from poor dental health - they are known among veterinarians as "toothless wonders". They enjoy long walks on the beach and spooning.

Pug

Happy   Jolly   Thrilled   Elated

Joyful   Convivial   Upbeat   Merry

Exultant   Delighted   Content   Pleased

Cheerful   Ecstatic   Playful   Introspective

The Many Moods of Pugs

Ah, the Pug. Known as the "Husband Substitute" breed for its tendency to snore, grunt, wheeze, and put on weight. Between its brachycephalic condition, enlarged floppy soft palate, and a narrowed trachea, this dog spends a good portion of its life passing out. Their playful nature comes from chronic hypo-oxygenation leading to a perpetual endorphin high. The fossil record is incomplete so no one knows how the Pug came into existence and they aren't talking. One story has Pugs warning the Dutch in the 16th century when Spanish invaders approached. This has been inflated with every telling over time and the truth is much less impressive. The Royal Pugs were awoken from a deep slumber by the smell of chorizos that the Spanish soldiers carried in their packs. Thinking they were getting a special treat, the Pugs used their limited supply of oxygen in an unprecedented level of wheezing vocalizations, thus "warning" the Dutch prince. Another historical story has the British misinterpreting how well the Pugs were treated at the Peking Imperial Palace. Thinking that they were valuable, British soldiers sacked the palace, leaving everything else behind except the Pugs. As seen with how the English dealt with the terrier breeds, they couldn't leave well enough alone with this one either. Thus, they made the fawn-colored Morisson Pug, named after The Doors' lead singer and the black and coffee-brown toned Willoughby Pug, after Abner Willoughby, inventor of the self-adhesive stamp.

Yorkshire

Above, a "cut-out" of a Yorkie's coat showing tread-like locomotion ability

The Yorkshire is another breed originally designated as a terrier that was later watered-down and reclassified into the toy breeds due to its uselessness. The last time they ever had actual jobs was in the 19th century, keeping mines cleared of rats and used in hunting (yeah, I know, hard to believe). One of the difficulties they encountered in accomplishing these tasks was when the bows used to keep fur out of their faces kept snagging on things at inopportune times. They are known to hate children, not liking to share the spotlight with what they consider inferior beings. Like the Maltese they have rotating treads rather than legs, seeming to glide along effortlessly even over rough terrain. Their curtain of fur hides these treads that require much less maintenance than other breeds, needing to be changed out only every two years or 3,000 miles by a trained veterinarian.

They make good long-term constant companions. This behavioral make-up, however, makes them emotionally unstable. Think Glenn Close's character in the movie *Fatal Attraction*: "I'm not gonna be ignored, (name of owner)!" An owner should never, ever lose physical contact with them as they will automatically start pining. They should also certainly never be left alone, as they will act out because of your absence, resorting to graffiti, pyromania, and "cutting" themselves. There is often a misunderstanding of terms when someone refers to this breed as a therapy dog. What they really mean is that this breed requires a lot of therapy.

A Yorkshire that "breeds true" has no fewer than twelve hereditary diseases.

The Australian Silky Terrier is another attempt to fool people that it is a divergent breed. It's just a Yorkie that uses conditioner.

Shih Tzu

Often confused with Lhasa Apsos, some people will tell you that Shih Tzus are smaller. However, when their average sizes overlap, the other way to tell the difference between them is this: Lhasas bite, Shih Tzus don't. That's also why you won't find Lhasas in the toy breed section. Lhasas - not a toy. You can also view this breed as a less messed-up Pekingese, as those are in its genetic background as well. This dog, even among toy breeds, is considered a major suck-up. Described as happy, outgoing, and trusting toward all, they will go off with anyone who gives them attention. Their name comes from the ancient martial art of Shih Tzu practiced by Tibetan monks. At the height of their popularity, the Empress Tzu Hsi coddled them and fed them shark fin, curlew liver, and antelope milk. As far as contemporary Shih Tzus are concerned, it's all been downhill from there. This forces owners to try too hard in attempting to please them.

Brussels Griffon

Comes in both rough and smooth coat varieties. Its facial expression is just an external representation of its disapproving nature. They were first shown in Brussels in 1880. The current population in Great Britain is a result of the Doggie Boom of breeding following World War II. They are known as great bluffers which comes in handy against larger dogs and in poker games. It is said that owners should be loving and tolerant as this breed is stubborn and hard to train. Griffons however find people very easy to train because of owners' loving, tolerant natures. Stripping must be done by a professional groomer, though it is difficult to find a groomer who also strips.

Non-Sporting Breeds

Bulldog

The genetic train-wreck of the dog world. This is such an unnatural animal that it is unable to give birth normally, but puppies must rather be delivered through C-section, though some have been done by the lesser known D- and E-section procedures. This form of delivery is only the start of many other corrective surgeries that will occur throughout a Bulldog's life. They are where the phrase "good personality" comes from. Whereas other descriptions give breed predispositions toward diseases and hereditary defects, for brevity this is the only one with a very short list about what _doesn't_ go wrong with them. Their earlier use was in bull-baiting. A Bulldog would be left outside a bull's stall at night and the dog's snuffling, snorting, wheezing, and gurgling would keep the bull awake, making it irritated and surly for the next day's fight. This is a great breed for wealthy insomniacs.

They are sensitive to heat, cold, barometric changes, exercise, excitement of any kind, the thought of exercise, movie plot twists, altitude changes of more than three feet, and life in general. Breeders will often minimize the negatives of this dog and are usually desperate to sell the puppies before the full range and effect of genetic defects kicks in.

This breed is an ironic icon of many football teams and the Marine Corps since it is completely incapable of any activity more vigorous than listening to NPR. Mascots at games and events will always be attended by a veterinarian and an emergency response team, oxygen tank and mask at the ready.

Boston Terrier

Not only known for its distinctive black and white markings but has a bark particular to its region of origin: "Bahk! Bahk! Bahkbahkbahk!" Like a lot of the brachycephalic breeds, its friendly nature derives from a poorly oxygenated brain. Their bulbous eyes act independently of each other, allowing the adaptive ability, as seen in many prey species, of being able to see a full 360 degrees around them. This trait was immortalized in the Kim Carnes 1970s song "Steve Buscemi Eyes". One of the few breeds indigenous to the United States. In one of many, many political blunders, the Boston was declared the state dog of Massachusetts during Michael Dukakis' governorship. One of the most famous Boston terriers was Samuel Adams' dog, Scooter, the first to board English ships in the 1773 Boston Tea Party raid. Tragically, in the colonist's zeal, Scooter was accidently thrown into the harbor and lost amidst the barrels of tea.

Chow Chow

This is the only breed that, like sharks, is able to bite as soon as it is born. It is so named because it will chow down on just about anything that moves across its vision. They come accompanied by an extremely thick coat so you can't bite back. Euphemisms used for this dog are "reserved", "suspicious", "aloof", "quiet loner", "standoffish", "keeps to themselves".

Aggressiveness seems to be intimately tied to its long list of genetic defects in that if you are trying to breed for the "look" of the Chow, you will invariably and inevitably evoke its "temperament" as well. Considered "non-sporting" as they will resist anything asked of them that they do not wish to do and often resort to subterfuge and underhanded tricks. It is said they were used as food in China, though this was more as retribution for biting their owners. How this dog is not extinct today is amazing. Attempts have been made since 1887 to develop a more sociable Chow. No luck so far. Good dog for testing reflexes and sprinting times.

Dalmatian

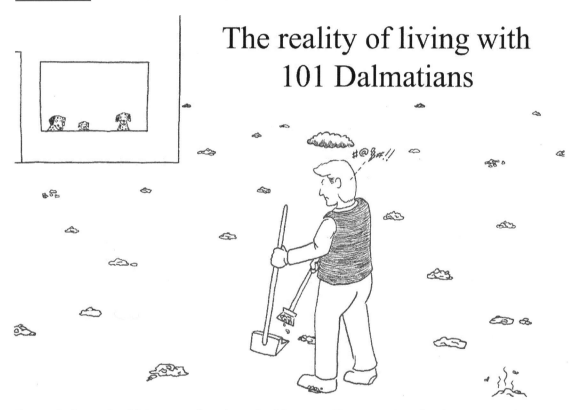

Known in its earlier history as a "carriage dog" because they were too dumb to <u>not</u> run between the wheels, they later became the stereotyped Firehouse mascot. Its hyperactive nature keeps firemen awake during their shifts. They only have two speeds: 4th gear and dead. They are incapable of having a linear thought, so training is just about impossible, which is another thing that keeps firemen busy during slow work times. They are fondly referred to as "Damnations". Born white, a relatively benign, symbiotic dog-pox virus causes their distinctive black spots to form at around two weeks of age. This pox virus is not transmissible to other dogs. Rarely a Dalmatian will be born black with white spots and in Slavic mythology this is a sign of prosperous times ahead.

Spitz

"The Finnish Spitz has a significant lead,
however the Japanese Spitz still has a chance
at the silver. The crowd is quiet as the German
Spitz prepares to hawk a loogey......"

So-named for their bad habit of expectorating. Many individuals develop a taste for chewing tobacco. There are three main Spitz breeds, the brown, fox-like Finnish Spitz, the white Japanese Spitz, and the varied colored and sized German Spitz. There is actually so much variety in coat, color, and size amongst the "Spitz" designation that pretty much anything with a curly tail and enlarged salivary glands can be called a Spitz. The Wolfspitz, for instance, is also known as the Keeshond. The Eurasier is another Spitz-related breed that comes from crossing a male Chow and a female Keeshond; like mules and ligers, offspring of such breedings are infertile. The German Spitz has a self-cleaning coat by Amana. In the 1950s some breeders carried out a poorly planned inter-breeding program and came up with the short-lived Spitz-Spitz, which had such a viscous saliva that it digested itself, dissolving into a mucousy blob that went on to attack a small, mid-western town. Luckily it was defeated by its susceptibility to cold.

The Spitz "breed" dates back 6,000 years. Prehistoric representatives of these dogs had poisonous glands set right behind the angles of the mandible. Cave drawings of Stone Age peat dogs with the Spitz conformation makes them the oldest domestic breed to not amount to anything.

In the 70s there was a famous Spitz, named Mark, known for his phenomenal swimming abilities.

Lhasa

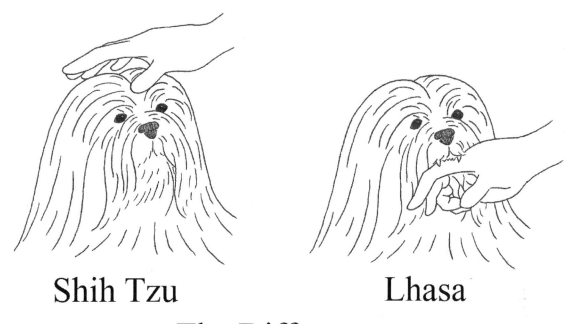

Shih Tzu   Lhasa
The Difference

A native of Tibet until monks could no longer tolerate or condone their stubborn and aggressive nature, this breed follows, instead, the teachings of Sun Tzu. The Dalai Lama gave four Lhasas (the last breeding pairs) to a traveler on an expedition, where they were ceremonially handed over rear-end first to the "Shagua", which translates as "fool" in Chinese. They can survive harsh climates and high altitudes; their tough background is what makes them so independent and opinionated. They only deign to allow humans to groom them since they themselves do not have opposable thumbs, yet they are not shy about telling people when they're done by biting them. The term "owner" and "pet" are reversed in Lhasa-human relationships. There are many myths surrounding Lhasas. Tibetans believe they are reincarnated monks that erred in a previous life which might explain their short temper at the vagaries of the universe.

Another belief is that a Lhasa will receive a person's soul at the moment of death. And eat it.

Poodle

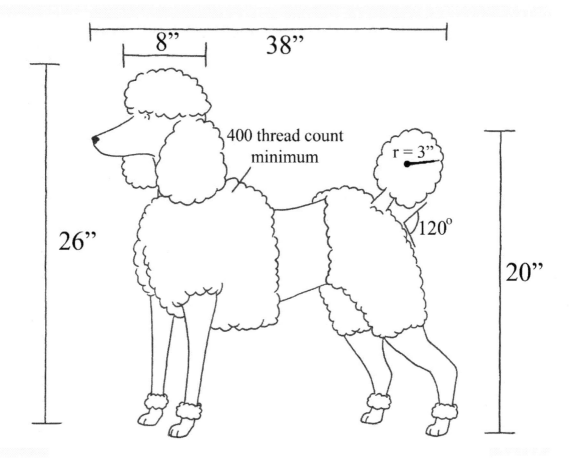

Above, the Standard Poodle: the Poodle by which all other poodles are judged

The epitome of the over-pampered pet. Germany has abdicated responsibility for this breed's origin since France took to sissifying it, dressing it in little outfits, developing an over-fondness for bows as accessories, and constantly rewarding its sense of entitlement. Another topiary dog, they come in many sizes: Standard Poodle, Miniature Poodle, Toy Poodle, and even smaller Nano- and Pico-poodles. This is another victim of poor hereditary dental disease, losing teeth faster than an outmatched ultimate fighter. They are considered the zombie breed of the dog world since they continue to live into ages unseen by other breeds regardless of what parts stop functioning or fall off. They come in so many colors, you can obtain swatches and find a poodle to match any possible home color scheme. Parti-colored poodles, however, are not allowed in show rings because such shows are taken very, very seriously.

In Goethe's *Faust*, Mephistopheles first appears in the form of a black poodle. Make of that what you will.

Substandard Poodles

Shar Pei

Above, the aesthetically-challenged Shar Pei

Another breed, like the Bulldog, that is sought after for its unique and multi-faceted genetic flaws. They have so many health problems that some veterinarians make a good living by having Shar Pei Only animal clinics. Their name, in Chinese, means "opposite of hybrid vigor". Used mainly for aggressive occupations, no one today seems to understand why it behaves the way it does. One way to view a Shar Pei is as a short-coated Chow. They were outlawed in China in 1947 because the Communists didn't want competition. Exported like other cheap crap in the 70s and 80s, they became other people's problem, like swine or avian flu. It has a prickly cactus-like coat to further endear itself as a household pet.

Schipperke

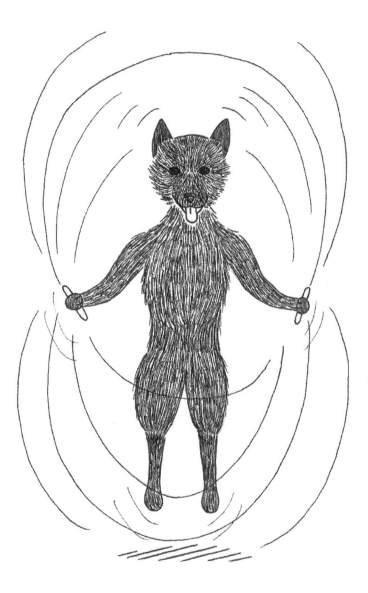

Named for its unique carefree skipping gait. Known as tireless, they remain unbeaten in jump roping world competitions and hold the record for longest jump roping time without a rest. It is essential to keep them away from caffeine and other stimulants as they are prone to spontaneous combustion. Their continual movement keeps a perpetual static charge in their thick coat. Scientists have been attempting to harness this as a cheap source of renewable energy. They do have one unfortunate and unpredictable trait leftover from their background as a barge watchdog in that they may bite and attach themselves to the genitals of newcomers to homes or even their owners. People interested in this breed should keep this in mind along with the word "tireless".

General

"Non-sporting" is the nice way to say that these breeds were found to be unacceptable to any of the other categories. Sort of like the "Island of Misfit Dogs". Another, kinder, term some use for these dogs is "Utility breeds" because some of these breeds were once useful in various functions. But, no longer.

Other members in this group include the devout Canaan Dog. Any prospective owner must be apprised of their yearly pilgrimage to the Holy Land. The Kromfohrlander is just a fancy German name for "mutt dog". The Tibetan Spaniel and Tibetan Terrier are further examples of how little monks have to do in the monastery other than develop new dog breeds.

Mixed and/or Fake Breeds

Curs, mutts, and mongrels are often ignored when talking about dog breeds, as if they're the bastard sons of the king with no claim to recognition. Whether you call them "mixed breeds" or the more legitimate and intentional sounding "cross-breeds", they are the definition of the phrase "the heart knows what the heart wants". Yet, the so-called "pure breeds" are just glorified mutts with combination of breeds in their backgrounds. Don't let anyone tell you different. When dogs are allowed to breed indiscriminately - the way they want - what you eventually end up with is a mid-sized brown dog. Some of these dogs make as perfectly a good choice of pet as a pure-breed, unless you've got a lot of fox-hunting, badger baiting, or rat catching that needs to be done by a dog with a good resume. One definition of a pure-breed dog is a dog that you pay more for. Let's face it. How difficult is a "breeder's" job to put two horny consenting dogs in a room together? What exactly are you paying for? It's not like they're doing advanced multi-level genetic allele testing to create the best Lab or Boxer. In some ways, because of what is "favored", they may even be selecting for known genetic defects (see Bulldogs and Shar Peis specifically but many others certainly qualify). If you were to weed out enough negative traits, some of these breeds would virtually disappear. Mixed breed dogs may have better genetics due to hybrid vigor and a diluting effect of negative traits. So, unless you have a specific need for a sheep herder or a good CPA, you might want to consider a mixed breed.

Now we get to what I call fake breeds. Fake breeds are mixed breeds that people are trying to pass off as superior "real" breeds. The Labradoodle is the most well-known of these. They're mutts with cutesy, marketable names. The theory touted about fake breeds as opposed to your common plebian mixed breeds is that you get the "best" of both breeds without the negatives. Yeah. Right. Because that's how genetics work. No. It's just as likely that you're going to get the hip dysplasia of Labs coupled with the luxating patellas of Poodles and wind up with a four-year-old dog who's had three surgeries and still doesn't walk right. It's almost guaranteed that people are going to mess this up. The other marketing ploy with these breeds is that it seems like regardless of which two breeds you put together, they become magically hypo-allergenic. I call that kind of dog the Abracadabradoodle. They're also called "designer" dogs and breeders really need to get away from this wording because it makes it sound like these dogs are put together by children in third world sweatshops for pennies a day. Next thing you know, Martha Stewart and Kathy Gifford will be trying to get in on this action. The whole fake breed phenomenon is a shell game for "breeders" to make an even easier buck. It's unfortunate that people fall for such tactics. Even if I allow for letting some "breeders" off the hook as earnestly trying to generate good genetic stock, this whole thing has opened the door for anyone to throw any two dogs together, portmanteau their names, and charge hundreds of dollars for the privilege of owning a "designer" dog. Some examples:

Chihuahua/Yorkie - Chorkies, which unfortunately sounds like some form of erotic asphyxiation; also called the sexier sounding Yorkihuahua

Pug/Beagle - the Puggle combines the stupidity of one dog with the low intelligence of another and you end up with nasal passages that cannot process oxygen fast enough for their hyper-excitability winding up with a dog who passes out in its search for food

Pomeranian/Poodle - usually called a Pomapoo, since Poodleranian sounded too "Middle Eastern", because the world needed another form of fluffy useless dog

Boston Terrier/Pug - the Bug comes by its name not only by combining the two but also as a description of its cranial capacity; puts a lie to any claims of making a better breed, because what could possibly go wrong with breeding two severe brachycephalics together, except to cave-in their heads

Jack Russell/Poodle - the Jack-A-Poo or Jack-A-Doodle because we just can't decide which is the cuter name!!!!!!! Either way, trust me, the Russell part will completely dominate the wussified Poodle genes and you won't see much difference.

Labrador/Poodle - the ubiquitous Labradoodle is touted, as weirdly many of these combinations are, as "hypoallergenic" or "non-shedding" or "non-allergenic", as if, unlike all other mammalian life, they don't have any coat loss or turn-over; look, if you're allergic to dogs, get a cat

Labrador/Mastiff - the Mastador, they should really be called Labrastiffs since their hips will go bad around six months of age

Chihuahua/Bichon - a Chi-Chon (pronounced She-Shon); this breed sells seashells by the seashore.

Maltese/Yorkie - Morkies are not actually a fake breed like the others, but instead hail from the planet Ork and are hell-bent on Earth's destruction - beware!

Cocker Spaniel/Poodle - the Cockapoo combines the worst skin conditions of the first with the poor dental and musculoskeletal system of the latter, but with the extended lifespan of the Poodle component, you get to take your pet to the veterinary clinic more often for a longer period of time

Golden Retriever/Poodle - besides sounding like something that only pees and poops, the Golden Doodle is not the name of an Asian food restaurant, rather it's a longer coated Labradoodle; again, the myth perpetuated here is its "allergy friendly" nature because Retrievers are not at all known for shedding (if you're unsure if the previous comment is sarcasm, just ask your nearest Golden Retriever owner)

American Bulldog/Neapolitan Mastiff - sounding like a virtual reality dog from the Matrix, the Neo Bull takes another step into absurdity, as if you couldn't just combine any Mastiff with a Bulldog.....nooooooooooo.......it has to be the Neapolitan so the name comes out right

American Eskimo/Australian Shepherd - The Australian Eskimo. Why? Except for the cognitive dissonance factor, what would be the purpose for doing this? At all. Someone should really be going to hell for this one. You end up with the dog that doesn't know whether to pull or herd a sled.

Chow/Labrador - The Chabrador. Another "why?" breed. As in, "why would you do something like that to the nice Lab?"

Chihuahua/Dachshund - Called the Chiweenie because no other combination did really well in focus groups; what you get is a faster, meaner, longer, biting dog for all of the cuteness of its name

Chinese Crested/Yorkie - Called a Crustie. Sounds like something you'd want, doesn't it?

Schipperke/Poodle - A Schipperpoo. Not with those knees it won't.

Schnauzer/Poodle - A Schnoodle. Right. Because taking the hypothetical "non-shedder" breed and combining it with the "allergy free" breed makes it "Ultra Allergy Free!" It's all in the name, folks.

Miniature Pinscher/Pug - Called a Muggin or a Puscher, either way this combination is up to no good.

Rottweiler/Poodle - Rottipoo. The name exudes cuteness, like a charming nickname. "Who's my little, Rottipoo?" They will, however, kill you.

American Eskimo/Shiba Inu - The Imo Inu, an angsty breed into softcore punk music.

Chihuahua/Pug - Called the Chug because of its propensity toward heavy drinking after seeing itself in a mirror

Pekingese/Poodle - The Pekapoo. Once you get it home, it will go and hide and never be seen again.

Alright, alright. Enough. I could go on, but I won't. Except for one last thought. What, at all, is the purpose of combining ANY of the small, fluffy breeds together. The Maltipoo, the Bichonese, the Peke-A-Tese (I'll let you do the work on that one), the Shihtzpoo (okay, I made that one up, sorry, I'm getting punchy over these names). Anyway, you just get the same basic looking small, fluffy breed. It's ludicrous. Besides people getting ripped off, I object to these fake breeds because it takes further attention away from legitimate mixed breed dogs. The world did not need more people breeding more dogs of whatever pureness and/or variety. There are plenty of dogs to go around without people interceding. When someone is asking you to shell out hundreds of dollars for one of these fake breeds, make sure to ask them why you should pay so much for what is basically a mixed breed dog. Truly, why should you pay so much for a pure breed dog at that? Again, not a lot of quality control or effort going into a great final product. You can find some pretty good dogs, maybe even some that look suspiciously like a Pekapoo or Labradoodle down at your local animal shelter. Look, when it comes down to it, there are really only two breeds of dogs: good dogs and bad dogs. And there are plenty of good dogs for everyone.

As an aside, the strangest pairing I have ever heard of was a Bassett Hound/Chinese Crested combination. Now, I don't know how this would happen, but I'm thinking alcohol was involved.

Dog Bathroom Positions

I had to include this section. Let me emphasize. I *had* to. My only defense (besides insanity) is for me to refer you to the introduction where you were warned that this book goes places that no other dog breed book dare go (just like dogs themselves). Keep an open mind. You may learn something about your own dog by way of the following illustrations. Or not.

Dog Bathroom Positions

Male Traditional

(Masculine Female Non-traditional)

Female Traditional

(Feminine Male Non-traditional)

The Sprinkler

Prone to just spin one way then abruptly change directions. Not known for their fastidiousness.

The Cirque du Soleil

So named for their acrobatic tendencies. Basically just show-offs.

The Over-Achiever

Over-extends to get just
that much higher.
Males only.
Primarily small breeds.

The Idiot

No matter what they do they
end of peeing on themselves.
Also males only.

The Walker

Just like it sounds.
Feels the need to walk
while going potty.
Maximizes area owner
has to clean up.
Universally despised.

The Center

Similar to the Walker, this
is a football position term
where the dog stays in one
place but feels the need to
alternately lift their feet
off the ground while going.

The Centrifuge

Sniffs and sniffs and sniffs
and spins and spins and spins
until the owner loses patience

The Thinker

Usually seen going out to yard
with the morning newspaper
or latest issue of Dog Fancy.

Miscellaneous Dog Cartoons

What you'll find in this section are a bunch of cartoons showing dogs and their people at their best and worst. Some of the cartoons are idea expansions on breeds or other sections of this book. Every once in a while, between groups of cartoons you'll find some Fun Facts! that you can share with your friends and show how smart you are. Enjoy!

Dogs have never been known for their higher reasoning abilities

grrrrrrr.....

And you call yourself
a working breed!

****

MOTHER!!

...and this is her before
her ears were cropped and
her tail docked.

Xena's mother always found
new ways to embarrass her

Joe's new Retriever
proved to be somewhat
of an embarrassment

****

He just never seems happy.

Fun Fact! The average dog owner accidently ingests a half-a-pound of fur per household dog per year!

****

****

Fun Fact! While the majority of dogs are known to help people's health by increasing the person's activity, walking more, and decreasing stress, 25% of dogs have also been known to cause decreased health in their owners by raising their blood pressure through misbehavior, being underfoot at the wrong time (say....at the top of the stairs), or committing an owner to more exercise than their heart, lungs, or musculoskeletal system are capable of!

Dog Telepathy

****

Good thing he has a nice personality to compensate.

****

Fun Fact! The tallest dog was a Great Dane that measured 44 inches (48 inches in heels) and was responsible for the demise of the world's smallest dog, a bite-sized Yorkie that stood 2 1/2 inches tall!

Fun Fact! Owning a dog (of any size) decreases the chance of home burglary! Owning a dog increases the chance of your home looking like it was burglarized!

****

Fun Fact! It is said that dogs don't see color, however that is not true! Their retinas have fewer cones, therefore they see a limited spectrum of color! So, they have relative color-blindness, which makes them useful in Human Resources departments in reviewing job applicants!

I agree we should work on his biting behavior. However, I don't think that should be our first concern here.

Oh, please....
don't tell me.

It's a
Pugasus!

****

We named him
"Speed Bump".

How do you expect a French Poodle to kiss?

****

Fun Fact! One dog and her offspring can produce 66,000 puppies in six years! Your dog will hate you for allowing this, because not one of their children, grand-children, great-grand-children, etc. will ever call or visit!

Chihuahua Nightmares

****

Fun Fact! The Drooling Breeds such as Blood Hounds, Mastiffs, and the St. Bernard produce up to ten gallons of saliva a day! They are only capable of swallowing one gallon a day!

Fun Fact! You can tell your dog is lying to you when their paws sweat!

****

I want him neutered, but
my dog won't allow it.

"Oh, don't worry.
He's over 21 in people years."

Using his owner's fame, George Washington's dog became known as "Father of Our County"

****

****

Fun Fact! Kubla Khan was a hoarder reportedly having 5,000 dogs at one time!

Fun Fact! Bluey, an Australian Cattle Dog, is listed as the oldest dog at 29 years 160 days, though veterinarians urged euthanasia for the last four years of his "life"!

Fun Fact! Whether a dog's nose is wet, cold, dry, hot, arid, tepid, temperate, moist, freezing, humid, or balmy has nothing to do with the dog's health, either positively or negatively! If you believe nothing else in this book, believe this! No, no. Really. I mean it. See, no exclamations.

****

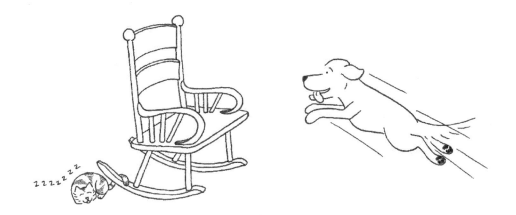

"And the beauty of it," Charlie thought,
"is that it will look like an accident!"

"I'm a Shar-pei, but you wouldn't know
it by looking at me. That's because I use
Wrinkle-Away skin cream! Now as a
bath lotion too!"

Every dog is surprised when they're reunited with their testicles in heaven

****

I say! Isn't that Pavlov's dog?

I have a name, you know!
It's Bob!
Not that anyone asks!

Pavlov's dog long resented not getting the name recognition his owner did

****

Fun Fact! Dogs have 1,700 taste buds, half of which are devoted to distinguishing the many flavors of poop!

Fun Fact! Alexander the Great named a city in memory of his dog, Mr. Ruffles!

He listens better to my husband.

****

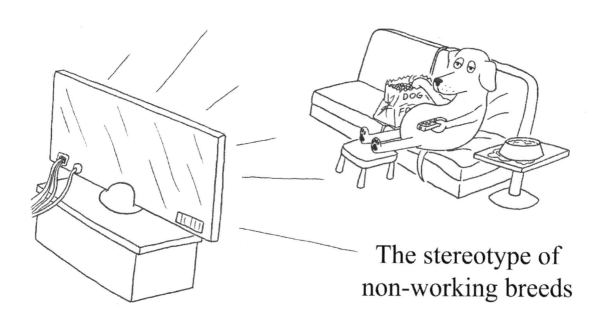

The stereotype of non-working breeds

****

Breeding for cult tendencies

Hare Vizslas

Dog Dates

****

I've been breeding for years!
Since this is a rare trait,
it's going to cost you extra!

****

Looks like what you have
here is a Max Pin.

Fun Fact! 33% of dog owners _will admit_ to having conversations with their dog, leaving phone messages on the answering machine while they're away, buying them presents, signing the pet's name to greeting cards, including them in family pictures, and/or saying such things as "sorry", "excuse me", or "thank you" to them! 99% of dog owners actually do all of the above!

Fun Fact! The fastest dog is the Greyhound which can achieve speeds over 40 miles per hour! The slowest? It's a tie between the Norwegian Plodder and the Arkansas Mosey Shepherd!

Fun Fact! Dogs have excellent night vision, so, yes, they see what you're doing in the bedroom there!

✳✳✳✳

It took months of on-line courses, but I finally got _my_ Master's degree! So. Who's the master now?! Say it! Who's. The master. Now?

Being a puppy, Rex didn't quite understand
the concept of marking his territory.

****

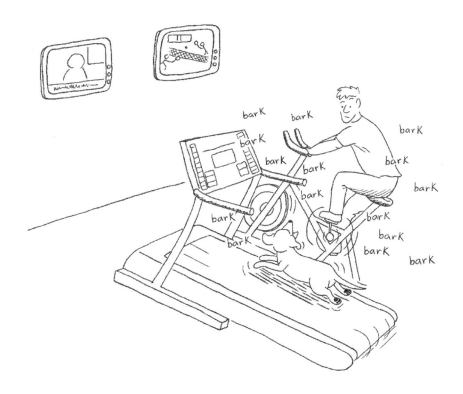

****

Look, little dude. Open your
eyes! The collar is just the
Man's way of keeping us down!

It would appear you left your Chocolate Lab out in the sun too long.

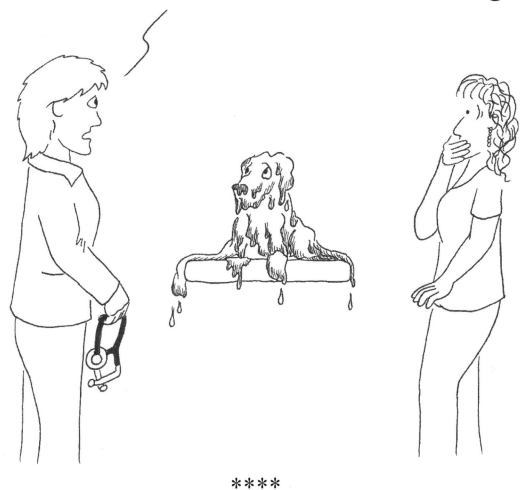

****

Fun Fact! In a 2010 survey, 75% of dogs said they practice Zoroastrianism!

The breeder told me they have very few medical problems.

****

Fun Fact! One female dog and her progeny could produce over 66,000 puppies in as little as 6 years! Which means nothing to stupid people who don't spay and neuter their dogs! It seemed worthwhile to mention this twice!

Fun Fact! Dogs are mentioned in the Bible 14 times! Cats? Zero.

The party was going well until Misty did "Choo Choo" across the carpet

****

Has anyone seen the cat?

****

Superman's dog, Krypto, could leap tall
fences in a single bound!

142

****

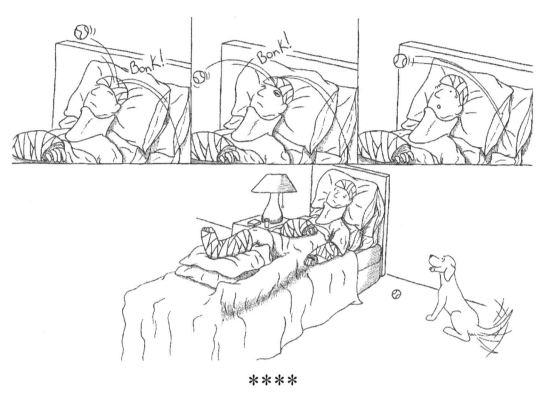

****

Dachshundkwondo

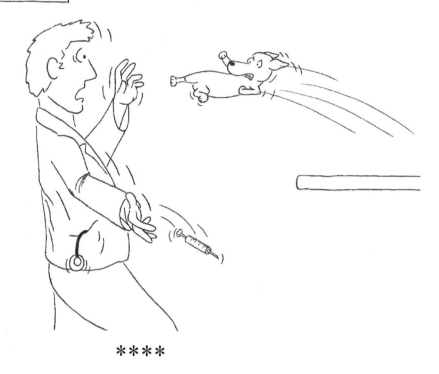

****

Fun Fact! Obesity is the number one owner-induced health problem among dogs!

Fun Fact! Studies have shown that dogs have no sense of time and is the reason for their chronic tardiness and poor stand-up comedy!

Fun Fact! A human nose contains about 6 million sensory receptors and we choose to smell roses! A dog's nose contains 200 million sensory and they choose to smell.....well, not roses!

Fun Fact! A dog can locate the source of a sound in 1/600th of a second and can hear four times farther than a human! So, yes! They hear you, it's just, sometimes, they don't care!

Fun Fact! Dog nose prints are as unique as human fingerprints! Which is helpful when you want to figure out exactly who ate the steak off of the table, slobbered on the cat, or knocked over the floor lamp!

Fun Fact! Two dogs make a pack! Three to five dogs make a passel! Six to nine dogs make a peck! And ten or more dogs make a pile! Lots of piles!

****

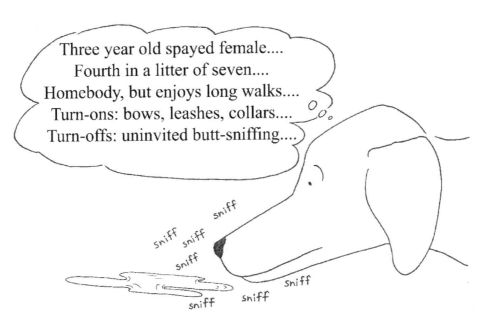

Dogs get a lot of information through smells

"Gets it from his mother's side of the family - she's half-Labrador, you know."

****

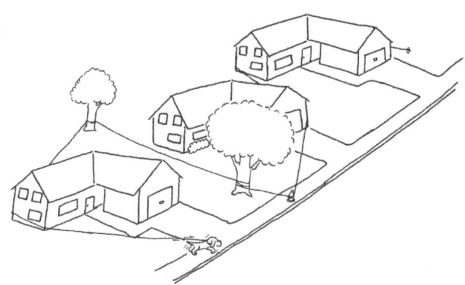

No matter how long the leash, a dog will always be found at its farthest length.

He's a new breed.
They're very good with children.

****

Mom, Dad.......I like cats.

Death's Dog

He's a rare Belgian Chipoodlyormaltitzu! Mr. Barnum, the breeder, let me have him for only $1,000!

****

Fun Fact! It has been documented that some dogs have learned up to 300 words, though the word "No" continues to stump many!

Fun Fact! There are 400 million dogs in the world! There are 7 billion people! There are a little over 6.5 billion sad, sad, people!

Piranha Dogs

****

Toto, being neutered, never got his
wish granted by the Wizard.

Reservoir Dogs

****

"I have a special offer to make just for you!"

Carl had a dog for every occasion

Your great-grandfather was a pitbull! Your grandfather was a pitbull! I'm your father and I'm a pitbull! But, _**you!**_ You want to be an **accountant!**

****

Is everybody ready?

Acknowledgments

Acknowledgements for inspiration need to go to The AKC's World of the Pure-Bred Dog edited by Duncan Barnes and the staff of the American Kennel Club; The Ultimate Encyclopedia of Dogs, Dog Breeds, & Dog Care by Dr. Peter Larkin and Mike Stockman; The Dog Encyclopedia by Drs Dominique Grandjean and Jean-Pierre Vaissaire; Legacy of the Dog by Tetsu Yamazaki and Toyoharu Kojima; and The Illustrated Directory of Dogs by Juliette Cunliffe. A special thanks to Duane Stamper for bringing his editorial acumen to the material and having it make sense. Continued, more nebulous acknowledgements go to the decades of dogs and dog owners I have seen or been told stories about that form the great majority of the material in this book. Thank you for your unwitting assistance! Special thanks, as always, must go to my wife and family for putting up with all of the time and neuroses that go into projects such as this.

About the Author

Dean Scott is a legitimate veterinarian, at least the last time he looked. He graduated from Arizona State University with a Bachelor of Science degree in Zoology in 1987. After doing four years of hard time at the University of California, Davis School of Veterinary Medicine he was released on his own recognizance in 1993. His business cards identify him, therefore, as a BS,

DVM. He has been funnier longer than he has been a veterinarian and five years in the Army didn't fix that. He currently maintains a population of two dogs and two cats in his household, always preferring to have an equal balance of power to keep everyone honest.

On the cover: Iggy (2003 – 2016), our Labrashund or Dachador, if you will. I use to refer to him as a Teacup Lab. He was the laziest dog in the world; then when we found out he had hypothyroidism, we felt a little guilty for the insult. Later he got cursed with Cushing's disease also (named after the late actor, Peter Cushing), which helps not at all with your physique or your good looks. Food must have been involved in taking this picture because that was the only time he really shined. Shine on, Iggy!

Made in the USA
Columbia, SC
24 June 2018